# STUDIES
## IN
## I CORINTHIANS

# STUDIES

IN

# I CORINTHIANS

BY

RUPERT E. DAVIES

WIPF & STOCK · Eugene, Oregon

Wipf and Stock Publishers
199 W 8th Ave, Suite 3
Eugene, OR 97401

Studies in 1 Corinthians
By Davies, Rupert E.
Copyright©1962 Epworth Press
ISBN 13: 978-1-60608-719-0
Publication date 5/6/2009
Previously published by Epworth Press, 1962


Copyright © Epworth Press 1962
First English edition1962 by Epworth Press
This edition published by arrangement with Epworth Press

THIS BOOK
IS GRATEFULLY DEDICATED TO
MY WIFE

## CONTENTS

|  |  |  |
|---|---|---|
| | NOTE OF EXPLANATION | 9 |
| | INTRODUCTION | 11 |
| STUDY ONE: | DIVINE AND HUMAN WISDOM<br>$1^{1-9, 18-31}, 2^{1-16}, 3^{1-4}$ | 19 |
| STUDY TWO: | THE UNITY OF THE CHURCH AND THE GIFTS OF THE SPIRIT<br>$1^{10-17}, 12^{1-31}, 13^{1-13}$ | 27 |
| STUDY THREE: | THE WORK AND AUTHORITY OF THE MINISTRY<br>$3^5-4^{21}$ | 41 |
| STUDY FOUR: | THE CHRISTIAN ETHICS OF SEX<br>$5^{1-8}, 6^{12}-7^{40}$ | 49 |
| STUDY FIVE: | THE CHRISTIAN AND HIS BRETHREN IN HEATHEN SOCIETY<br>$6^{1-11}, 8^{1-13}, 9^{1-27}, 10^{1-33}$ | 63 |
| STUDY SIX: | WORSHIP AND RESURRECTION<br>$11^{1-34}, 14^{1-40}, 15^{1-58}$ | 75 |
| | QUESTIONS FOR DISCUSSION | 93 |

## NOTE OF EXPLANATION

THESE ARE substantially the Bible Study addresses which I gave during the World Methodist Conference at Oslo in the summer of 1961, and (in a slightly different version) to a Summer School for Methodist Local Preachers just before. In spite of their Methodist origin, I do not think that they have a particular denominational flavour. It was necessary to make some alterations from the spoken version, in the interests of grammar and style, but I have kept such alterations to a minimum.

Instead of going straight through the epistle, I have brought together in each study the passages which refer to the subject of the study, and I believe that this makes for a much better understanding of the epistle as a whole. I have assumed the use of the *New English Bible* throughout, but the reader will find it very profitable to have other versions as well beside him.

I am very grateful to Mrs Y. O'Connor and Mrs F. E. Webb, who wrestled successfully with the difficult task of reducing a tape-recording to an intelligible typescript; to Mr Brian Brooks, who supervised the original tape-recording operation; to my daughter, Mrs Mary Sullivan, who has greatly helped in the preparation of the typescript for the Press; to Mr David Foot Nash and my wife, who made such careful notes of my addresses that I have been able to correct the obscurities of the tape-recording from their transcripts; and to the members of my very responsive audiences who asked me to try to have these talks published.

Good commentaries on 1 Corinthians are not numerous. I owe much to the one written in *The Christian Students' Library* by my friend, W. B. Harris.

RUPERT E. DAVIES

DIDSBURY COLLEGE
BRISTOL
JUNE, 1962

# INTRODUCTION

THIS LETTER of St Paul to the Corinthians contains some of the most appalling revelations. When I first studied it, as a boy (I think it was for an examination), I don't think I really believed that what St Paul said had happened in Corinth had really happened there. In a sense I believed it, because on the whole I was inclined to believe what St Paul said, but it did not register in my mind that Christian people could be guilty of the things of which they were guilty according to St Paul. They were guilty, as we shall soon discover, of quarrelling, of intellectual arrogance, of drunkenness at the Lord's Supper, of litigiousness, and even of incest and prostitution. That was a pretty large list, I thought. Certainly I didn't believe that Christians *since* the time of Paul, whatever may have happened in his day, had ever done things of that kind at all, and if it had been suggested that Christians of my own time (which of course was to me the most important time of all) had done them, I should have frankly contradicted the statement.

But experience has made me, I hope, a little wiser on this matter. It is my business to study and read and talk about Church History, and I am bound to say that I discover in Church History, and not least in the higher councils of the Church, some of the things which St Paul referred to; and I am bound to say that I think that the Church today is not entirely guiltless of them, not perhaps as actual things committed outwardly and notoriously, but as tendencies to which the Christian Church is always subject, as temptations to which from time to time it yields. And because of that, because the things that St Paul talks about are always present either under the surface or above the surface in the life of the Christian Church, and not least today, it is extremely important for us to study the First Letter to the Corinthians. It not only brings before us the truths of the Christian faith, which it certainly does, but it draws our attention to those weaknesses and temptations to which we are always liable, and from which no Christians who have any humility about them can ever claim to be permanently exempt. So please from the start let us avoid any mood of self-righteousness which may creep over us, and agree, even against our present opinion, that even we might be liable to some of the things about which St Paul speaks. Not all of them, I hope, but some of them, according to our circumstance and temperament. This, to me at any rate, makes this letter particularly relevant and contemporary.

Of course, the sins to which the Corinthians were liable were very largely, in their *form*, derived from the pagan environment in which they had been brought up, an environment from which they had been in principle liberated, but from which they had not yet entirely freed themselves. You could hardly have expected them to have done so in ten to fifteen years! There were stages in the development of character and in the development of their common life out of which they had not grown.

And indeed Corinth was a very pagan city indeed; there was no more typical example of a pagan city in the time of St Paul, for almost everything pagan happened there. The Corinth which some of you may have read about in earlier Greek history was a very notable city, in some ways a more notable city than the one we have to talk about. It was very important politically and culturally and strategically. You have in your minds the map of Greece. This map will consist of two parts joined by an isthmus—in fact, I imagine the isthmus of Corinth is a capital example of what is meant by an isthmus in a geographical text-book. Now on the isthmus, or actually slightly south of the isthmus, is the ancient city of Corinth. When cities in the north of Greece were fighting the cities in the south of Greece, a very frequent occurrence, Corinth was a very important ally, and each side wished to have it among its supporters. And from that point of view Corinth was extremely important always. It also had a culture of its own and a city life of its own which are worthy of a place in any history of Greece. That city was destroyed by the Romans two hundred years before the time of Paul.

But a hundred years later it was built again: Julius Caesar set up a Roman colony on the site of the ancient Corinth. No, not quite on the site of the ancient Corinth. The ancient Corinth was on the slopes of a tremendous massif, called the Acro-Corinthus. In my more vigorous youth I once climbed almost to the top of the Acro-Corinthus, and I know enough about that massif to know how grim and forbidding it is. The city was built on the slopes, overlooking on the one side the Saronic Gulf, and on the other the Gulf of Corinth. So you could see both North Greece and South Greece, and the eastern sea and the western sea. That was the ancient city of Corinth.

Slightly below that Julius Caesar set up his colony. Now a colony in Roman times was a very ingenious method of imperial administration. You put Roman citizens to live in the middle of a foreign country. They were possibly native Romans, more possibly they were non-Romans who had fought for Rome and had been honoured by Roman citizenship; there they lived with the full rights of Roman citizens, and the opportunity to take Roman baths, and to enjoy Roman holidays, and to live the Roman way of life in the midst of the non-Roman people who lived around them. It was a means of spreading Roman civilization and protecting Roman interests in other countries. That was the Corinth of St Paul's day, a Roman colony—a very important outpost of Roman administration.

It was also the capital, as you will remember, of the Roman province of Achaea, and the place where the governor of that province lived. It had great commercial importance by reason of its geographical position. All ships with cargoes from Asia Minor for Italy, if they were wise, made use of it. They could of course sail around the south of Greece, but that was a long and stormy voyage; what they did much more commonly was to come to Corinth, unload their goods and go back to where they came from. The goods were then taken over the isthmus by various means of traction and loaded on to a ship on the other side, and from there the goods would continue their voyage. Sometimes, in fact, in certain critical periods of Greek history, ships had actually been pulled themselves over the isthmus. But that was not the normal way of proceeding. Corinth was thus the place where two sea-roads met, and the commerce of the city was extremely important and extremely flourishing.

The life of Corinth met and matched the commercial nature of the site. I don't wish to show any disrespect to those who come from Southampton or Liverpool or Newhaven, or any other notable port, but you will know what I mean when I say that ports tend to collect the riff-raff of the population of the world. And so you found in Corinth not only very respectable and pompous Roman citizens, but also a great number of other sorts of people—thousands of slaves, of course, and small shop-keepers, and, I suspect, a large number of brothel-keepers, public-house keepers and lodging-house keepers. I have no doubt if you went round certain parts of London the clergyman or minister on the spot could show you the present parallel to Corinth.

It also had another importance. The real centre of Corinth had been, right through the history of the ancient city and of the new city, the Temple of Aphrodite. Now Aphrodite is the goddess of Love, and in the Temple of Aphrodite there was a resident staff of a thousand prostitutes, and there was an expression in Greek '*Korinthiazein*', which means 'to spend a weekend in Corinth'. There is also an expression about 'spending a weekend in Paris', which has something of the same meaning. And the Temple of Aphrodite in Corinth, of course, was a centre of attraction in all sorts of senses. It gave the city of Corinth its character, its fame, its notoriety, and much of its manner of living. You must not, I think, dismiss Corinth just as a city of vice. Remember that in the ancient world, as indeed in certain parts of the modern world, the cult of sexual love had a sort of religious quality. From our point of view that may not even seem possible, but there is a kind of religion, a *natural* religion, that you find in the Old Testament as well as in Corinth—and I think you find in certain circles today—a cult which, as it were, deifies the sexual relationship, and sometimes not without a certain nobility and creative possibility. D. H. Lawrence was the prophet of such a cult. That is the sort of thing that went on in Corinth, together with the other more disreputable manifestations.

Paul came to Corinth on his first stop from Athens. In Athens he had, you will remember, preached to the intellectuals, and it is generally supposed—I am not sure that it is quite certain, but it is generally supposed—that he was not very successful. At any rate there is no evidence of a Christian Church being immediately founded. It is possible, therefore, that Paul came to Corinth with a certain feeling of disillusionment. Things went much better there than they had done in Athens. He preached at first in the synagogue, as he nearly always did; but quickly he turned his attention to the Gentiles. Among the Gentiles his work was successful, and a Church was very quickly established. That caused jealousy on the part of the Jews, who went to the governor of Achaea, Gallio, and told him that Paul was an obnoxious person and an enemy of established order. Gallio, as we are told, 'cared for none of these things'; but we must not think that he was not interested in public order. The phrase means that he saw the Jews for what they were. They were just making trouble for someone they didn't like, and as it was a mere matter of dispute between two sects about an obscure religion, he, Gallio, was not going to do anything about it; and in fact he did nothing. The Jews went away with their tails between their legs. It was at Paul's own time that he decided to go on from Corinth and preach in other places. He left the city and the Church to proceed according to his judgement, but no longer under his direct guidance.

Soon after he departed a man called Apollos came. Apollos is a rather mysterious figure, I always think, in the New Testament and people are still writing books about him; nobody can quite say what his beliefs were and what he said, but the general impression made upon us by the New Testament is that Apollos had been a follower of John the Baptist, that he had been baptized perhaps by John the Baptist or one of his followers, and afterwards became interested in the teaching and life of Jesus. He gave his audiences at first a mixture of John the Baptist's teaching and the teaching of Jesus. He did this in the city of Ephesus, and among his audience were Priscilla and Aquila, converts and friends of Paul, who took him aside, as people do sometimes take a preacher aside, and told him what he ought to have said. On this occasion Apollos was more willing to listen to what members of his congregation told him he ought to have said than preachers sometimes are, and when Priscilla and Aquila told Apollos that Jesus was the Messiah, that He fulfilled the expectation of John the Baptist and that it was He of whom John the Baptist had spoken and whose way the Baptist had prepared, Apollos was persuaded that this was true, and so he proceeded from a sort of partial Christianity to a full Christianity, and became an eloquent preacher of the Christian faith. He was particularly useful in conversing with the Jews. He knew the Old Testament Scriptures inside out, and wherever he went he was able to argue with the Jews on the merits of the claim of Christ to be the Messiah. It was to do this that he came to Corinth and there he continued the work of Paul and continued to build up the Church. Then he also continued his travels.

After he had left, things in Corinth did not go so well, A decline in Christian understanding and in Christian love set in, and Paul, hearing about this, sent to Corinth a letter, not the letter we have here (the First Epistle to the Corinthians is in fact the second one that Paul wrote), but one that we haven't now got. He wrote this letter, and nobody seems to have taken much notice of it. That, by the way, often happened to St Paul's letters. I think we take more notice of them than the people of Corinth did! That may be a comfort to us, because we ourselves—like St Paul—often cannot know what good we are doing; even when we think we have been quite useless and hopeless in our efforts, to judge by immediate results, in fact the Spirit of God goes on working, and He continues to work long after the immediate effects of our efforts have spent themselves. At any rate this letter of St Paul's had no apparent effect, and as he continued to travel he received even more disquieting news about the Church in Corinth. It came to him from news sent to him by a lady called Chloe, a leading lady in the Church of Corinth. Members of her household came to him in a body and brought the message from their mistress that things were in a poor way and would he please do something about it. At about the same time as he had the message from Chloe, there came a letter from the Church in Corinth asking for his advice on various matters, and it is in response to these reports from the household of Chloe and the letter which came to him from the Church in Corinth that Paul wrote the letter which we have in front of us. That is the kind of background against which the letter was written and against which it needs to be understood.

Now for some dates. Paul probably came to Corinth in the first place about the year A.D. 50, rather late in that year, and stayed there until perhaps the spring of 52. He wrote this letter which we have in front of us perhaps in the spring of 55, three years after he had left the city. That gives you some notion of the distance from the time of the Crucifixion, which I suppose we ought to date about A.D. 28, to the writing of this letter.

STUDY ONE

## DIVINE AND HUMAN WISDOM
(1 Corinthians 1$^{1-9,\ 18-31}$, 2$^{1-16}$, 3$^{1-4}$)

**1$^{1-9}$.** In view of what Paul is going to say later on about the way in which the Corinthian Christians have behaved, it is a little difficult to understand how he could ever have written these verses. He is thanking God for all their virtues, and the cynic might say that he is doing so in an ironical spirit—thanking God for all the virtues they *think* they possess. But I don't think that is his idea at all. I think he is perfectly honest and sincere, thanking God for the Christian progress of the Corinthians, and with equal sincerity assuring them that Christ will keep them firm in their faith until the end, in spite of their bad record in the past. He can say these things because of the phrases: ' To the congregation of God's people at Corinth, dedicated to him in Christ Jesus, claimed by him as his own ', or as it says in the Revised Version, ' sanctified in Christ Jesus, called to be saints '(1$^2$). There are here two phrases which give the key to what St Paul can say about the Corinthians.

First, there are the words usually translated ' saints ' and here translated by the phrase ' claimed by him as his own, dedicated to him in Christ Jesus '. The Corinthians have this bright future before them, the Corinthians have these graces and virtues, because, and only because, they are dedicated to God. They are set apart by God, they are made over to His service, they are part of His very own people; and although they may disgrace themselves, although they have the greatest difficulty in living up to the wonderful expectations formed of them, and although they are poor Christians indeed, yet they still are set apart by God, and they have that mark upon them which makes it quite certain that they will be preserved at the end by Christ Jesus. I don't mean that they can't possibly fall away, but I do mean that in spite of their disloyalty, failure, cowardice and everything, Christ has set His mark upon them and will not let them go, and if they are separated from Christ it will certainly be by their own choice. That's the first thing; they belong to Christ Jesus and they will therefore be kept safe to the end.

The other phrase that makes it possible for Paul to say these things about the Corinthians is—'in Christ Jesus'. I want to draw your very special attention to that phrase. If you are preachers you have read it from the pulpit; but if not, you have read it in your own private devotions, and you have heard it read to you hundreds and thousands of times, I have no doubt whatever, because the phrase 'in Christ Jesus' occurs, in one form or another, several hundred times in the Epistles of St Paul. It is one of his habitual phrases, so habitual that you probably don't take any notice of it. You think that it is just one of the ways in which he talks. But it isn't, and in St Paul's writings 'in Christ Jesus' contains a very large amount of his Gospel. I want to try and explain what he means by it.

The human race, according to St Paul, can be divided into two classes: those who are in Adam and those who are in Christ. If you are in Adam you belong to the corporate body of humanity, sharing the heritage of Adam, living according to his principles, and being jointly responsible with all the other members of the Adam class for the sins which they commit. Of course it is not our fault that we are in Adam; after all, we were born into Adam, we are natural members of the human race. And of course this talk about Adam doesn't mean necessarily that there was one human being called Adam. 'Adam' stands for the sinful, unredeemed human race, and most people are members of the human race 'in Adam'. But the rest of mankind, a rather small number, but a growing number, are 'in Christ'. And as Adam stands for the human race before the time of Christ, Christ stands for the human race as it is redeemed by Him. To be 'in Christ' means to be transferred from the solidarity of humanity to the solidarity of the Church of Christ, and to be in relationship both with Him, with Christ personally, and at the same time with all those who belong together with you to Him. The phrase 'in Christ' is a description of a personal relationship with Jesus Christ and also of a communal relationship with all God's people. And that's what a Christian is; he is 'in Christ', he has been transferred from the 'Adam community' to the 'Christ community', and he is personally related both to Christ and to all his fellow Christians. Christ is the Head, we are the body; we all belong to Him and we all belong to each other. Now the Corinthains, for all their defects, are 'called to be saints', set apart for God's special purpose; they are 'in Christ', and therefore Paul can thank God for them, and he can express his deep conviction that they will be firm in the faith.

This is another way of saying that Christians lead a double life. These Corinthians certainly led a double life. They were still semi-pagan, their emotional development was extremely stunted, they were by no means free of the old rivalries and jealousies and hatreds; but they were also 'in Christ', they were advancing in faith, they were appropriating the good things which God had in store for them, they were becoming holy. We can see how both those things can be true if we realize that they are probably true of us. We also are not yet integrated, not yet mature. Nevertheless, there are two things going on inside us: the old nature is at work, though, we hope, it is gradually being subdued and purified; the new nature is developing and maturing under the power of the Spirit. We lead a double life, and we are no better than the Corinthians, nor indeed do we in that respect need to be or want to be better than the Corinthians, because we know it is part of the common destiny of mankind to have these tendencies towards evil, and also by God's grace we have available to us the power of Christ in the Spirit. As Luther so often remarked, we are both 'justified and sinful', and becoming holy is not a miraculous event by which we pass immediately from awful sinfulness to complete holiness. It is growth in grace, progress under the power of the Spirit.

**1¹⁸⁻³¹.** The next verses, which we are not at this moment going to consider, 1¹⁰⁻¹⁷, go straight in at the deep end. Paul can hardly restrain himself during the first nine verses from talking about the evil things which are happening in Corinth. As soon as he has got to the end of his thanksgiving he goes for the Corinthians hammer and tongs. But for the present we will go on to 1¹⁸, and in the verses from there on Paul explains to them why the party spirit he has mentioned is rife among them.

This quarrelling which has broken out in Corinth is due to the false claim to wisdom which the Corinthians are making. The people of Corinth were no doubt 'intellectuals'. We know the word and we know what it means! They were versed in Greek philosophy—not, I think, in Greek philosophy of the highest and most profound sort, which had mostly died out in Greece, but in the base forms which had now been passed down for generations and still flourished. These intellectuals had not fully understood that when Christ came their pretensions to wisdom would have to be given up. So Paul draws quite plainly and quite sharply the distinction between human wisdom and divine wisdom. The distinction which he draws is this: human wisdom is the attempt of the human mind to find out all about God without aid from God Himself (I don't think that is a fair description of all types of philosophers, but it does represent some kinds of human thought; it is an attempt to reach the being of God by speculation on the nature of things); divine wisdom is what comes down from above, comes to us by revelation, giving to us the truth which we cannot obtain by working through the processes of our own minds. And, said Paul, it is divine wisdom, and not human wisdom, which is to be found in the Gospel. Human wisdom at its best, he says, is a poorer thing than even the divine wisdom at its worst (an odd way of putting it, but it serves to emphasize the distinction between the two things), and he points out that in order to make that quite clear to the world, God has chosen non-intellectuals, lowbrows, people of no kind of birth or even respectability, as the agents of his Gospel, and so there is no place for pride in the presence of God. 'You are in Christ Jesus by God's act, not by your own wisdom.'

I think that this brings us up against one or two things that we ourselves might otherwise be prone to. I think we all assume—don't we?—that people who count in religion in the last resort are clever people. Perhaps we wouldn't admit to thinking that, especially if we don't believe ourselves to be clever people, but we have a sort of unconscious respect for clever people and perhaps we let them have the last word on difficult matters of the faith. What St Paul says contradicts such a view. The other danger is a more subtle one: it is that of assimilating the Gospel to theories we have already embraced. I shouldn't think that anybody in this room has not done that! You see, we pick up certain kinds of theories from the world in which we live, probably the current psychological, political, or philosophical theories. They become part of ourselves. Then we read the Gospel and make it fit in with what we ourselves have already decided upon. That is a standing temptation to every thoughtful person. It is a point where simple people have the advantage over those who think, because they haven't got any thought-out theories. They are humble at the start, but we are not. We bring to the Gospel what we think the Gospel ought to say, or, in more practical terms, we know what we want to find in the Gospel and find a text afterwards to fit it. Paul gives a very clear warning against that. If we take him seriously, we shall have to examine a great number of our presuppositions. We often hear people say: 'Christianity is democratic, isn't it?' But the question is not whether Christianity is democratic, but whether democracy is Christian. The same applies to the American and the British way of life in general. All kinds of presuppositions that we drink in with our mother's milk (or, if that is not strong enough, that we take from our Sunday newspapers) become part of our daily thinking, and we do not always permit them to be judged by the Gospel. We are to judge our theories by the Gospel and not the Gospel by our theories. That goes for us, and also, it may be suggested, for Rudolf Bultmann, who, for all his great spiritual insight, has really accommodated the Gospel to modern Existentialism.

**2¹⁻¹⁶, 3¹⁻⁴.** Paul points out the characteristics of divine and human wisdom, and shows us the contrast between the two. Four characteristics of divine wisdom stick out a mile.

Firstly, divine wisdom is a mystery. I don't think the word 'mystery' actually occurs in the *New English Bible*, but it occurs in the older versions. It is in many ways a very useful word, but a word that can be so easily misunderstood that I imagine the *New English Bible* people decided to omit it. But we can use it. Paul had a special meaning for it. It isn't a mystery in our sense at all. The word is taken from the religious language of the times, the language of the ' mystery ' religions; and in the ' mystery ' religions, which were secret societies with a strange religious life, a mystery was what you learned when you were initiated, and you were not allowed to disclose it to anyone. There were many sorts of ' mysteries ', mostly designed to assure people of immortality. The nearest parallel today is the secret lore of Freemasonry. Paul liked the word ' mystery ', and he says, ' we have a " mystery ", but our " mystery " has been revealed; it was treasured up in obscurity within the confines of a particular nation in a dark form, but now at last the mystery is out, divine wisdom is revealed to mankind '. You may remember the engagement of Princess Margaret. That was a mystery in the proper sense, concealed from the Press, and the public—until the right moment. But when the Queen, or whoever it was, decided the time had come for the news to break, it did, and the truth was out. Now God's mystery is the same sort of thing, kept dark until the right time, and then it was out. And that is why Jesus is our wisdom; the mystery of divine wisdom is revealed, and human salvation is disclosed, and everybody can have it. So there isn't, after all, anything of the secret society about it; the mystery *was* concealed and now is revealed.

The second characteristic of divine wisdom is that it is

displayed in the Cross of Christ, in the death on the gallows of a man condemned for treason, and this event is the centre of all Christian preaching. This is not the time to expound the meaning of the Cross of Christ. But notice—Paul lays it down as quite essential that any gospel that is preached which is not centred in the Cross of Christ may be an excellent gospel, may be very well suited to the contemporary situation, but it is not the Gospel committed to the Christian Church.

Thirdly, this mystery, this wisdom, can be revealed in its fullness only to those who are mature in the faith. The truth can and must be preached in a simple form to outsiders, and it is by such preaching that they are first brought on to the early stages of Christian understanding. But the fullness of it comes only to those who are mature, and therefore the wisdom of God is not revealed to quarrelsome, jealous people, because they have stunted their own growth by their foolishness and selfishness. Only if you are prepared to be open to the Spirit of God, who will mature you in understanding, only then will the wisdom of God ever come to you in its fullness. You can't have the wisdom of God on the cheap. You must be prepared to learn from the Spirit the meaning of grace, and to fit yourself for the impartation of His wisdom; otherwise you will no doubt be saved, you will no doubt be forgiven, you will no doubt be justified, but you will remain an infant in arms as far as the divine wisdom is concerned.

Fourthly, the divine wisdom is taught by the Spirit; it is a *spiritual* wisdom. There is no word more mangled in Christian use than the word ' spiritual '. When we say a thing is ' spiritual ', a sort of holy hush descends upon the audience and the processes of thought are brought to a standstill. I sometimes think it would be better if we avoided it altogether. But the word ' spiritual ' in the New Testament really does mean something. It means ' that which is imparted by the Holy Spirit '. I think that it always means that. The wisdom of God is spiritual, taught by the Spirit. It goes home to men's hearts and consciences by the power of the Spirit; otherwise it won't work at all. The Spirit in St Paul, as I hope we shall go on discovering throughout this letter, is not a vague influence. The Spirit is a Person who knows the mind of God, who knows the depths of God's mind. There is no thought-out doctrine of the Trinity here, or even of the deity of the Holy Spirit. But such doctrines are made necessary by what we are told here, because the Holy Spirit is here described as a Person who imparts his personal wisdom to persons, who guides our minds, who moves our hearts and who is our companion in life; and it is by the agency of the Holy Spirit, understood in that sense, that the wisdom of God comes home to us. Once we have got hold of the idea that the Holy Spirit teaches, we shall have no doubt that He is a Person; for teaching, real teaching, is an intensely personal activity.

$2^6$. The divine wisdom is 'not a wisdom belonging to this passing age, nor to any of its governing powers, which are declining to their end'. Here Paul gives us a glimpse of his philosophy of history. There are two ages in human history—the present one, and the one to come. But in Christ the coming age has already arrived, and Christians are living in it. Yet the present age still continues, though its 'governing powers ... are declining to their end'. These 'governing powers' are the demonic forces in which Paul most firmly believed. He made them into malign personalities; we prefer to regard them as the evil forces in the mind of man which drive him towards destruction and war against his will. In either case the Gospel asserts that they have been defeated by Christ, and no one needs to obey them.

STUDY TWO

## THE UNITY OF THE CHURCH AND THE GIFTS OF THE SPIRIT
(1 Corinthians $1^{10-17}$, $12^{1-31}$, $13^{1-13}$)

$1^{10-17}$. Bogus wisdom leads straight to divisions in the Church. You can see clearly how it happens when one particular party or clique, or one particular group of Christians, claims to have a superior knowledge, to have the answer to this or that problem, and gives it out that its members know better than others. Of course there will form in the other part of the Church another clique which claims to have an even better answer, and so on, and before you know where you are the Church is divided. It can quite easily happen in a Conference or Summer School; it certainly happens in Churches.

The first place where we know it happened in Christian history was in Corinth. It took the form that each party claimed for itself the authority of this or that great teacher. It is quite clear that the members of it did not write to the teacher and ask whether he would sign the document they had drawn up, or be President of their society, or anything of that sort; they just took his name. Those in the first group said: ' I belong to the party of Paul.' So those in the second group said, ' I belong to the party of Apollos ', who was, of course, in many ways a more learned man than Paul. That made things difficult for the third party, for of course Paul and Apollos were the two great leaders so far, but then there was Peter (and Peter may indeed have visited the Church), and so they said, ' I belong to Peter's party '—or, as it here gives it, ' I belong to the party of Cephas ', the name of which ' Peter ' was the Greek form. The last party was rather longer in being created, but it said no doubt in its party broadsheet: ' We have duly weighed the reports of everybody else, and we feel that while the party of Paul has something to be said for it, and so also the parties of Apollos and Peter, we see the weaknesses in all these as well, and we are sure that the right solution is as follows, and we may therefore modestly claim to be the party of Jesus Christ Himself.' So each of the members said: ' I belong to Christ's party.' These people felt that they really were the goods—that they came out of the top drawer and that the others came out of various other places.

That is how it all happened, and Paul replies to it with devastating simplicity. So simple is the answer that the strength of it is often missed by those who read it. ' Is Christ divided? Has Christ been parcelled out among you?' 'The Church is one and indivisible because Christ is one and indivisible,' he is saying, ' and if you attempt to divide the Church, you are in effect trying to divide Christ. That is not only blasphemous but impossible. Surely Christ has not been divided out among you, you haven't all got a fragment of Christ '—and that is a particular smack in the eye for those who claimed to be of the party of Christ, the superior people, the really superior people.

I don't think we need say very much about it, for once that has gone home there is hardly anything more to do except to relate it to our own situation. The situation here described by Paul is not of course ours. These were the days before there was a divided Church. We live in the days of a divided Church. In Corinth there were considerable dangers, not yet realized, that the Church would split up into various groups; we live in a day when the denominations, the fruits of division, have existed for centuries. They have their own life and existence in history and tradition, their own vested interests, their ambitions too. There is a similarity, of course, in that many of the denominations are named after their great leaders, just as these Greeks name themselves after great leaders, but it is a different situation, and you may therefore say: ' Well, of course what Paul says to this little congregation of Christian people in Corinth does not apply to us.' But I draw entirely the opposite conclusion. If it is true to say to the people of Corinth, not yet divided, that they are attempting to parcel out Jesus Christ, how much more true is it, that we who have been divided for centuries, have tried to divide, to parcel out Jesus Christ! What was present as a threat in the time of Paul is present as a centuries-old reality in our time. What therefore applied to the first beginnings of division applies with very much greater force to our entrenched and inveterate divisions, and I do not myself see how a Christian reading this passage and understanding it can any longer for a single second look with complacency upon the divisions of the Christian Church.

It is of course, as I know well, possible to defend the existence of all the denominations. It is certain that there are tremendous obstacles in the way of Christian reunion and a great number of problems that have to be tackled, and that only some of them have so far been attempted. But it is quite self-evident that the object of our enterprise should be the unity of the Church, the resolution of our differences, and the giving up of the attempt to divide Christ up and parcel Him out among us. And when we take that into conjunction with the kind of world situation in which we are living, the imperative to Christian unity becomes surely even more compelling. How can it be desirable, possible, reasonable for us to be continuing our divisions when the world needs the Gospel in the way in which it does? And if we could for just a moment compare the things which divide us with the things which unite us, if we could for a moment reflect on the things which cause us to keep redundant chapels open or our Churches independent, and compare the reasons which we bring forward to justify these with the need of the world, and the broken unity of Christ's Church, I think we should see that we are somehow a bit one-sided and unbalanced in our thinking. That's all really I think I need say about these verses.

Possibly, however, I should explain what may be a little obscure in the last two verses, the passage: 'Was it in the name of Paul that you were baptized?' Paul answers his own question by saying that he didn't make a practice of baptizing at all. He baptized two people, he says—and then he remembers somebody else he baptized and had forgotten about. He remembers him just in time, and says: 'There are a few people I have baptized, but my practice is not to baptize. That is the business of other people; my business is to proclaim the Gospel.' The point he is making here is this: 'I don't want you to think for a moment that I am the centre of the Gospel; the centre of the Gospel is Jesus Christ. And in order that you should not think that for a single second, I have avoided even the practice of baptism.' What he said of himself he would have said also, I imagine, of Apollos and Cephas. The whole point, therefore, of these sentences is to underline the truth that the centre of the Gospel is not any man, but Jesus.

**12$^{1-31}$.** Although it is not until Chapter 12 that Paul begins his full-scale answer to Christian division, he has given his answer in principle in that single sentence—'Is Christ divided?' His full-scale answer appears in Chapters 12 and 13, provoked by a question which was raised by the Corinthians in their letter to him. They have asked him about 'the gifts of the Spirit'. This idea of the gift of the Spirit is an important one. Any translation I can give you will be a bit watery. There is a special word in the Greek which means 'the free gifts of God's abundant grace', gifts showered by the Holy Spirit on believers, gifts of different kinds for different purposes. They are the gifts of God's *grace*, beyond our deserts, beyond our most strenuous efforts, and they come to us simply by the goodness of God. The original Greek word is '*charismata*', closely connected with the word for 'grace'—'*charis*'. These Corinthians wanted to know which were the more important '*charismata*', to find out, if possible, if the one they had was more important than the one that other people had. It was all very human, and very much like us. Which is the more important, the Minister, or the Sunday School Superintendent? That is the sort of question they asked. They had been arguing about it, probably in their debating societies, and Chapters 12 and 13 are the answers that Paul gives to the question. You will see one or two other questions here referred to which came in the same context of questions, but the main question is the one I mentioned.

The answer of Paul is plain. All the various gifts come from the same Spirit, who gives to every man in the Church his own work to do and his own gift for the purpose. Some preach, some teach, some have a marvellous gift of faith. You may think it a bit odd that faith should come in the list of special gifts, because, of course, faith is the common gift of all Christians. I think it means that some people have a *special* gift of faith. They have the kind of faith that, when everybody else is doubting, remains staunch. You know such people. Some, then, have a special gift of faith, some heal the sick, some are good at administration.

Some, moreover, have the gift of ecstatic utterance—what we usually call the ' gift of tongues '. Now this is a great source of puzzlement to all of us. What is this matter of ' speaking with tongues ' in the Acts of the Apostles and the Epistles of Paul? The first thing about it is that the gift of tongues on the day of Pentecost is probably not the same as the gift of tongues here referred to. If you look at Chapter 2 of Acts carefully, you will see that it is really a description of something different from what we have here. On the day of Pentecost men and women could understand the apostles though they did not know their language. This is not quite the same. It seems to have happened in the early Church that under the influence of strong emotion people would cry out in the middle of the service in language which was very difficult to understand, and sometimes no doubt was a foreign language, and sometimes just unintelligible chattering. It seems a well-attested phenomenon that under the stress of strong religious emotion people will utter things which as far as we know they have never heard. We have parallels to this in many religious Revivals—in the time of Wesley, in the time of the great Welsh Revival at the beginning of the present century, and so on. You and I probably, with our sophisticated and critical attitude, are a bit doubtful whether it is a gift of the Spirit or not. We should think it just an emotional extravagance. Paul, however, regards it as a gift of the Spirit—but, notice, with reservations, as we shall see from other parts of the letter. The Corinthians thought it was the gift above all other gifts; if you could make that kind of noise you were obviously one of the saints. Paul puts it rather low down on the list, but he takes it as a gift of the Spirit, and includes it among the many gifts that the Spirit may give to us.

This, I think, throws light upon the strange verses at the beginning of this chapter: 'For this reason', he says, 'I must impress upon you that no one who says "A curse on Jesus!" can be speaking under the influence of the Spirit of God. And no one can say " Jesus is Lord!" except under the influence of the Holy Spirit.' Among the strange utterances which were heard during early Christian worship were apparently curses on Jesus, and salutations of Jesus as Lord. Paul is here saying that the mere fact that a man can produce an ecstatic utterance under the stress of emotion does not prove that he is inspired by the Spirit. You must test a man's utterances by the content of what he says. He is pointing out that the real thing that distinguishes inspiration from mere extravagance, or, for that matter, possession by evil spirits, is what the man says, and if he says, 'Jesus is Lord', it shows that his heart is in the right place; if he says other things you can't be quite so sure.

These, then, are the gifts of the Spirit. The answer to the question of the Corinthians is just this: these are *all* gifts of the Spirit, and we are not to regard any as more important than others. We are not to be proud because we have a special gift of oratory, or teaching, or learning, or administration, or even of faith, because we all belong to the one body and in the body we all have our function to perform; we all receive our gift by grace and not by our deserts, and our business is simply to fulfil our function to the glory of God, the building up of His people and the proclamation of His Gospel. All these gifts are the work of one and the same Spirit distributing them separately to each individual at His will.

Then follows the famous analogy of the Church to the human body. We may no doubt take it that St Paul was careful to consult medical authorities before he wrote his description of the human body, and so far as I can see he gets it fairly well right. What is very interesting, however, to us is not that, but his insistence on the unity of the human personality. There he is well in advance of his time. We nowadays talk very much about the unity of soul and body, but the ancients were not so concerned to do so. They were very careful to distinguish between soul and body, and often suggested that the soul could do one thing and the body another. Here Paul is quite clearly saying that the human personality is one. For remember that when he uses the word ' body ', he doesn't simply mean the flesh, that part which comes under the microscope, or could come under the microscope or the X-ray; he means the whole self. The unity of the human personality is for him the starting-point of his argument. Paul, then, describing the human personality under the name of ' body ', indicates how it all fits in together, and how every part belongs to every other part. If you remember all this you will see the great strength of his argument here.

Some people have said that Paul hadn't a sense of humour. But when he makes the point, ' If the body were all eye, how could it hear? ' I think that perhaps he hoped to raise a smile. It's a rather pleasant picture he has called up of a body consisting entirely of an eye, or an ear, or a nose. Clearly, if the whole body were one single organ there would not be a body at all! ' So the eye cannot say to the hand, " I do not need you " '. Next, he reminds us that some parts of our body are less honourable than others, and shows how we give them extra special attention. ' God ', he says, ' has combined the various parts of the body, giving special honour to the humbler parts, so that there might be no sense of division in the body, but that all its organs might feel the same concern for one another. If one organ suffers, they all suffer together. If one flourishes, they all rejoice together.'

In the last few verses Paul gives a list of the gifts of the

Spirit. Many people have taken this to be a list in order of priority: 'God has appointed, in the first place apostles, in the second place prophets, thirdly teachers; then miracle-workers.' I don't think that is the way in which it should be taken. The whole point is that all these gifts are the gifts of the Spirit, and we are not to be proud of any one that we particularly have. This is just the order in which they occur to him—apostles, prophets, teachers, miracle-workers, and so on. He does not mean that apostles are well away above all others, but that they are examples well-known to the Corinthians of the way in which the Spirit of God bestows His gifts. His point is not that one is more important than the other, but that we aren't all apostles, all prophets, we aren't all teachers, or all miracle-workers. There is an Old Testament passage which expresses the wish that all the Lord's people were prophets. I don't think that should be taken too seriously. We don't want everybody to be in the class of the prophets, or the apostles, or the teachers. There must be congregations as well as preachers, and the lay members of the people of God one of equal importance to the ordained members of the people of God. So in the body of Christ there is a gift for everybody and a place for everybody.

But in the thirty-first verse he appears to contradict this, by saying: 'The higher gifts are those you should aim at.' Which are the higher gifts? They are the ones that he hasn't yet mentioned! 'Now', he says, 'I will show you the best way of all'. If you read verse 31 in this chapter in the light of Chapter 13, you will see that the higher gifts are not these powers of teaching, administration, and so forth. They are the gifts of faith, and hope, and love. Those are the gifts we should aim at. Of those higher gifts of which you have just heard, the highest of all is love. And so Paul launches out on this the most famous of all his chapters—Chapter 13.

**$13^{1-13}$.** The Christians had a new word for love, the word 'agape'. They had to have a new word because they had a new conception and a new reality. There was a word for sexual love. That wouldn't do. There was also a word for friendship. Now the Greeks had a noble conception of friendship, partly no doubt because their conception of sexual love was inadequate, and because there was not, in Greek family life, friendship or partnership between husband and wife. It was natural that men should find their soul companions, their intellectual partners, and so on, among members of their own sex. That is one of the reasons why homosexuality was prevalent among the Greeks, and also one reason why, quite apart from homosexuality, they reached a high conception of friendship. But the word for friendship would not do either. It had to be a new word, and so the Christians took a word of rather neutral and unimportant significance, and filled it with this special content.

Books have been written about the Christian meaning of love, and no doubt you have preached and heard many sermons about it, and no doubt nothing I can say can add to it. But let us be sure to remember that, for the Christian, love starts in the nature of God; it is not a human achievement but a divine gift. It is *the* divine gift, because love is the nature of God Himself, and God is always pouring Himself out in love to His creatures. So love starts with God; it flows from God to us; and in response love is aroused within us; and the love which is aroused within us returns to God in gratitude, and flows out through us into our relationship with each other. The love which is aroused in us by the love of God towards us is in fact the same as God's love for us, taking its form from our human condition as it reaches us, but flowing through us back to God and outward towards our fellow men. That is something of the idea which Paul is here expressing, and which you will also find expressed in complete harmony with this in the First Epistle of John.

But Paul does not leave this conception of love in the air. It's very easy to make wonderful speeches about love, which people will applaud and which in fact get us nowhere, and so Paul was extremely practical about this. Do not let the beauty of his poetry blind us to the practicality of what he says. He tells us that love is not rude, he tells us that love is not selfish or conceited; and we all know enough about ourselves to know that this is a very practical application of the principle. He says that love does not keep any score of wrongs, doesn't gloat over other men's sins or the thought that Mrs So-and-So has done this and this and this that she shouldn't have. Righteous people have it, you know, as one of their special privileges, to feel how wrong everybody else is. There is a very famous passage in one of the greatest of Roman poets, Lucretius. It comes near the beginning of his great poem 'On the Nature of Things'. He says how sweet it is to sit on the shore of the sea, on the promenade, as it were, and watch the ignorant masses of humanity struggling with the waves and being drowned in large numbers. That is a very common attitude among enlightened people; it is an attitude to which we are tempted. We say sometimes: 'Look at so-and-so! See what has happened to him through not being a Christian!' We even excuse ourselves for reading the *News of the World* by saying; 'Well, of course, that's what happens to people when they don't come to church.' But love, says St Paul, does not gloat over other men's sins. Also, 'it delights in the *truth*'. And there is nothing love cannot face, there is no limit to its faith, its hope, and its endurance.

It's a guess, but I think an inspired guess, that when Paul speaks of love he is not thinking of love in the abstract, but of the embodiment of love as he knows it in Christ. You will see that if you put instead of 'love', at each point, the name 'Jesus Christ', you won't change the sense at all. 'Jesus Christ is patient; He is kind and envies no one. He is never boastful, nor conceited nor rude, nor selfish. He is not quick to take offence. He keeps no score of wrongs. He does not gloat over other men's sins. There is nothing He cannot face, there is no limit to His faith, His hope, His endurance.' So from one point of view this passage is a character study of Jesus Christ.

There are three things, says Paul, that will not pass away —faith and hope and love. Knowledge will go, because all human knowledge is partial knowledge and it will be lost in

Heaven in the vision of God. We shall know even as God knows us already. Prophecy, inspired preaching, will vanish away. There are no sermons in Heaven. The things that will last for ever are faith and hope and love, and the greatest of them all is love. Now there may be in your mind, as there is in my mind, a niggling doubt as to whether this is quite right. How can there be faith in Heaven, and how can there be hope in Heaven? I'm not sure if I know the answer to that. Let us try to see what it is in relation to faith. Faith after all is not mainly believing things which you cannot prove. That element of course comes into it, but faith is in its essence a personal relationship, the relationship of a man to his Saviour, of a child to his father, and that relationship, no doubt glorified, developed and perfected, will surely be in Heaven. How that applies to hope is not so clear to me. Can we say that hope, which looks forward to the future, and trusts implicitly in God's ultimate salvation, will be present in Heaven *in its realized state?* I'm not quite sure how that works out, and one of the things I look forward to in Heaven is Paul's communication of the truth to me in that matter. But for the moment let us see, as we can quite clearly see, that the greatest of them all is love. Love is not a transitory feeling, not a relationship of convenience and expediency and comfort; love is part of the very life of Heaven.

See how far we have come. We started off with this question of disunity, quarrelling, in the Church. We have seen it focused in particular on the problem of which gifts are more important. We have seen the solution, that all these gifts are gifts of the Holy Spirit to each one within the one body of Christ. And so we have been gradually enabled to see that more important than any intellectual or spiritual gifts is the gift of love. And there, of course, is our answer to the problem of unity—love—and the exploration of Christian love is the only way forward to Christian unity.

Just one additional remark about that. I think we all see that we ought to love our fellow Christians who belong to other denominations, and I would suppose that many of us have gone quite a long way in that direction. But I don't think that love in the Christian sense is limited to the relationship of one person to another. Of course it includes that, and it is most importantly centred in that, but surely it goes farther. Ought we not to see that Churches, congregations, denominations should love each other—that there is a relationship of what you might call corporate love in which Christian communities respect other Christian communities, are willing to learn from them, pray for them, seek the best things for them, and pray that God will grant to them those good gifts which He has already granted to us? So is there not in this principle of love, not simply a principle of individual conduct, but a principle of the relationships of congregations, denominations and Churches to each other?

One or two verses in this wonderful chapter perhaps require a little comment for our better understanding. ' If I am without love I am a sounding gong or a clanging cymbal.' The picture called up in the minds of Paul's readers when they read those words would be of a procession to the temple of a heathen god. We know that in the rites of Cybele, the great mother goddess of the East with her enthusiastic priests who mutilated themselves in the service of their mistress, it was the practice for the priests to go along the streets clanging cymbals and gongs—a meaningless, harsh, grating sound which nevertheless had the effect of working up people's religious emotions. If I'm without love, I am like that.

Then there is a famous argument about one of the verses here—verse 3—' I may dole out all I possess '—that's clear enough—' or even give my body to be burnt '. According to some of the Greek manuscripts here the second part should be, " or even give my body that I may boast ". There are two words in Greek that are very similar, with only one letter different, and the manuscripts give them both. I am inclined to think that what we have in the *New English Bible* is the correct reading, ' or even give my body to be burnt '. The reference may be to a famous memorial which St Paul may have seen in Athens. There came to the city of Athens some time before the time of Paul an Indian whose name was almost too long to mention, but the Greeks wrote it down as

Zarmanochegas. This Indian came as part of an embassy to Athens to ask for certain concessions and certain agreements with that city; and as he went through the city in solemn procession he suddenly threw himself on to a burning pyre with a smile on his face in order to show his devotion to his nation. He gave his body to be burnt, and this so much impressed the Athenian populace that they went to the length of setting up a memorial. If the other meaning is right, 'even give my body that I may boast', I suppose it may mean that a man might give himself away to slavery in order to boast how much he had given away for Christ—give himself into slavery to show how good a Christian he was. But all this is no good if we have no love.

STUDY THREE

## THE WORK AND AUTHORITY OF THE MINISTRY
(1 Corinthians $3^5$-$4^{21}$)

$3^{5-17}$. I think you will see that there is a fairly close relationship between this and the last study. The division of the Church in Corinth had plainly raised the question of the authority of Christian ministers. Can anybody get up at a meeting in the Church and say what he thinks is right? Or ought he to obey implicitly what the official teachers have said? In Corinth, you see, the party leaders got up and said: 'God has granted me a special revelation.' And somebody else got up and said: 'But Paul said something different.' What then is the authority of Paul? What is the authority of Apollos? Have the original teachers of Corinth the right to lay down the law for all time to come? What *is* the authority of apostles and of Christian teachers? The questions, and Paul's answer, refer to the ordained Ministry in general, not specifically to the apostles, but to all those set apart by the Holy Spirit for the teaching and preaching of the word of God, the accredited teachers and preachers of the Church.

The answer Paul gives is just a little bit complex, and in order to understand it clearly I must ask you to follow me rather closely. He uses three analogies—first of all, the analogy of a garden, then of a building, and then of a special kind of building, a temple. A garden, a building, a temple. First of all he describes the Church as a garden: 'You are God's garden', he says. Now in gardening, the gardener is important, and the under-gardener who does the watering is also important, but the really important person is God, because if it were not for God nothing would grow in the garden at all. Now the building. The man who lays the foundation of a building is very important, the man who draws up the design of the building is very important, the man who does the actual building is very important, but the all-important thing is the foundation. All the other people's work would be quite useless if the foundation were a poor one, or poorly laid. Then the temple. Of course, there also the builder and architect are important, but the all-important person is the God who is worshipped there.

Now let us apply the three analogies. The Church is God's garden: those who sow the seed and do the watering are important, but God is all-important. The Church is God's building; the builder and architect are important, but it's the foundation which really counts, and the foundation is Jesus Christ. The Church is God's temple; the builder and so on are important, but the all-important person is the the God who is worshipped there. In each case the important person is God—God the Father who makes the Church grow, God the Son who is the foundation of the Church, God the Holy Spirit who dwells in the Church. And there, you see, is the answer to the problem of the authority of Christian Ministers. They are God's agents, gardeners, builders; in each case what really matters is not they, but God. The only thing they have to look to is how well they do their work. The foundation is laid; they must build upon it with the right material. The seed is sown in the garden; they must be be very careful how they sow the seed and nurture the plant, but the responsibility is God's. The Church is God's garden, God's building, God's temple. Those three simple analogies save us from two dangers. First of all they save us from too high a doctrine of the Ministry—from supposing that the Minister is the person who makes the Church, that if there should be no Minister, there would be no Church. But the Minister does not make the Church. They save us also from too low a doctrine of the Ministry. Ministers are not just full-time servants of the Church. They are not merely convenient people to fill a pulpit or an administrative gap. Ministers are God's agents, God's fellow-workers (he even dares to say), workers in God's garden, workers on God's building, architects almost of God's temple. But the all-important person is not the Minister, but God.

From this I think that we may draw six principles about the Christian Ministry which are in Paul's mind:

(a) In the Church there are men—'planters', 'waterers', 'architects', 'builders'—whom God has chosen for the performance of particular tasks, and who are therefore set apart by the Church to do what God has called upon them to do. These are the ordained teachers and leaders of the Church—Ministers, if you like, with a capital M. All the Lord's people, of course, are ministers, with a small m. But the Ministers are those Church members, who, starting out as ministers, are recognized by the Church to be men whom God is equipping to be whole-time, set-apart Ministers in His Church, and whom the Church therefore trains, sets apart, and ordains in obedience to the divine will.

(b) The Ministry, therefore, is a Ministry within the ministry. It is a specific Ministry, but not a superior Ministry. All Christ's ministers remain under orders from above; each in his office, be it high or low, waits upon the divine will. One is the Master of all, and all remain brethren. But the Christian Church is not a democratic institution. The President of the United States derives his authority from the people. He is raised up from below. But not so the Ministers of the Church. They are called to their office from above. The gifts and graces, which are the evidence of that call, are also from above. The Church sets them apart and ordains them, not of its own volition, but in response to what it knows to be the will of God.

(c) Because the Minister's authority is from above, he is answerable, in the last resort, to God and not to man, because it was God who appointed him.

(d) The Minister must give a strict account of his Ministry, and all the more so, because he has to give that account to God, who appointed him, and not to man.

(e) The Minister exercises his authority rightly, and does his work properly, only if he builds on the foundation laid for him—that is, on Jesus Christ. By his fidelity to Jesus Christ his work will be judged.

(f) The Minister is not the overlord, but the servant and

pastor of the people of God. He is their servant in the sense that Jesus was the servant of His disciples. He is not the Church's employee, or someone it can order about because it pays him. Nor can he order the Church about. For Ministers and people are all under orders from God.

No Church can evade the duty of testing its Ministry by the standards laid down by Paul.

**3⁹.** We read in some versions, 'fellow-workers with God'; and in others, 'fellow-workers *for* God', or 'in God's service'. There are many people who think that to claim that we are fellow-workers with God is too big a thing to take upon ourselves and too bold a thing for Paul to say. Yet the whole argument of this passage implies that even the tremendous privilege of working with God is ours, and we can quite confidently accept this as the meaning of the words.

**3¹⁸⁻²³.** As Paul thinks of the pretensions of some of the upstart teachers in Corinth—these people who claim to have a wisdom superior to that of others and to that of Paul and Apollos—he is moved to remind them of the defects of human wisdom and the foolishness of human pride. The Ministers of the Church have all the resources of God and of the Church—quite true. But the Church belongs to Christ, and Christ belongs to God. There is therefore no room for pride, either in Ministers, however gifted, able, eloquent and successful, or in lay people, however obedient they may be to the word of God, however cultured they may be, however advanced in the knowledge and understanding of the word of God. There is no room for pride, for all stand under the judgement and mercy of God. The Church belongs to Christ, and Christ belongs to God.

**4¹⁻²¹.** In the previous chapter Paul has carefully explained the relationship of himself, as a Christian teacher and Minister, to God on the one hand, and to Christians on the other. He has shown himself to be an agent and a Minister of God, and to be a shepherd and servant of the Church. From the standpoint which he has now made very clear he deals with the criticisms—we don't quite know what they were—which had been levelled in Corinth against teachers and Ministers, not excluding himself. His reply to these criticisms is: 'I am God's steward. Therefore I am responsible to God and not to you. That is not something that I say just about myself; it applies to all the teachers—they are all answerable to God and not to you.' Perhaps that sounds like a high-hatted attempt to evade his proper responsibilities and obligations, but if we see Paul's underlying purpose in saying these things, that impression disappears. His whole purpose in these verses is to strip off from the Corinthian intellectuals the last remnants of their pride, their intellectual and spiritual pride, by showing them that everything they have—understanding, knowledge, faith, love—is a gift, the gift of God, not an achievement of their own. Therefore they simply have no right at all to sit in judgement on teachers who have come to them as God's ambassadors. Therefore he explains that he is responsible not to them but to God for his conduct, his teaching, his life. But even when he has said this, he is apparently still not quite sure that he has succeeded in undermining their pride. And so from this he breaks off in verse 10 into a passage of scorching irony. 'Of course, you clever people in Corinth have everything—I wish you had, then you could give us a share. We, your teachers, are a miserable lot—hounded from place to place, feeble, hungry, and in rags.' And then the note changes, from irony to appeal. 'I don't really want to shame you; I am trying to bring you to your senses. But don't run away with the idea that I am not coming to see you again, and that you can therefore carry on as you please, and have your own way and build a Church according to your own principles; on the contrary, I am coming very soon. The question is: When I come, shall I come in anger or gentleness?'

The Christian Minister, it is quite plain from these verses, has a task of discipline and judgement as well as of proclamation and pastoral care. The exercise of discipline and judgement is, in fact, a part of the exercise of pastoral care and a part of the proclamation of God's will to man. It is not the business of the Minister simply to 'keep in' with the congregation, to approve of what they do, to express what they believe. He must from time to time, stand over against them to announce the judgement of God, and to pronounce the discipline which God requires of them. That is a stiff task for a modern Minister in any conditions, and sometimes one that he knows he can exercise only with danger to his prestige, or even, in some Churches, to the position that he holds; but it is one from which he may not flinch, if he is to be true to his calling and truly answerable to God and not to man.

**4³.** 'I have nothing on my conscience' sounds a very arrogant thing to say just like that. Paul has sometimes been condemned for saying things of that sort. But if you go on to the next words, which belong quite clearly to these, you will find that he says, 'I have nothing on my conscience'; yes, 'but that does not mean that I am free from judgement; on the contrary, the fact that I have nothing on my conscience does not acquit me, for it is God who judges me, not my conscience.' It is also worth noticing that the word 'conscience' in St Paul nearly always has a sense rather different from our word 'conscience' in ordinary use. 'Conscience' in St Paul's letters is nearly always that inner voice which condemns us, not something which can either approve or disapprove of what we do, or advise us as to what is right or what is wrong, but something which comes into operation only when we do what is wrong. And so when Paul says he has nothing on his conscience, he means that he is not at this moment feeling himself condemned for any action which he has taken, or for any attitude he has taken up.

**4⁶.** 'Into this general picture, my friends, I have brought Apollos and myself on your account, so that you may take our case as an example.'

He means that he has used the names of Apollos and himself, in order to avoid invidiousness or hurting people's feelings, but what he says applies not to the case of Apollos and himself only, but to all the teachers known to the Corinthians, and to the relationship of such teachers to the whole Corinthian congregation.

**4⁹.** 'We are like men who are done to death in the arena, a spectacle to the whole universe.'

He means that the apostles are like criminals placed in the arena to fight against wild beasts, a Roman form of punishment for criminals and of entertainment for the populace.

**4¹⁹.** 'I shall take the measure of these self-important people, not by what they say, but by what power is in them.'

He means by ' power ', power for the destruction of evil. He will judge them (in other words), not by what they say about themselves, or think of themselves, or by the pretensions which they make for themselves, but by the power which they evince in their lives for destroying the evil which is in the world.

STUDY FOUR

## THE CHRISTIAN ETHICS OF SEX
(1 Corinthians $5^{1-8}$, $6^{12}$-$7^{40}$)

I think we all feel that when we approach the matter of sexual ethics we do not need to treat St Paul with quite the same respect as we do on other matters. We feel that he faltered a little as he spoke of such things, and we tend to regard him as responsible for some of the mistakes in that area of life of which the Church itself has been guilty, or which at any rate it has condoned. From that people sometimes go on to the sweeping assertion that St Paul is responsible for the misunderstanding of sexual life from his day until ours, which has corrupted the very springs of human life. That, perhaps, is not usually said by Christians, but it is often said more or less in those words by others who are non-Christians.

Christians and non-Christians usually have one thing in common in this matter—that they have not in fact read what St Paul has to say. I don't want to suggest at this point that St Paul has the answer to all our problems; I don't myself think he has. But I do think that we ought to do him the honour of reading him carefully, and considering carefully what he has to say. We ought to warn ourselves at the very beginning that our own practice in the matters of relations between men and women is not so admirable and excellent that it is for us to condemn others who have a different policy. It may be that we are so much enslaved by the practices and prejudices of our own time that we cannot clearly see what St Paul has to say to us. We are prejudiced against him from the start, because it suits our convenience and our custom to oppose him. With those warnings in our minds let us look and see what he actually says.

**5¹⁻⁸.** This is a matter which perhaps does not at present directly concern us. The man Paul is talking about here was living with his step-mother; it was a case of what we should call incest. St Paul is quite clear as to what should happen to the man in question. He should be brought before the whole company of the Church, and then he should be 'consigned to Satan'—which means presumably that he should be sent out of the Church, where Christ reigns, into the world, where Satan reigns. Now don't forget that St Paul believed that outside the frontiers of the Church Satan was still in control. His control was temporary, because his power had been smashed on the Cross; nevertheless he still reigned over that part of the human territory which had not yet been occupied by the Church. This man was to be consigned to that world where Satan reigns, so that his spirit might be saved on the Day of the Lord. It appears that Paul thought that if a man was thus dealt with he would have tremendous opportunity and incentive to repentance, having realized the consequences of his action. In the world into which he had consigned himself, he would be brought to repentance and so restored to salvation. This is therefore not a vindictive sentence on him; it is a sentence for his own benefit. This raises questions for the discipline of the Church which are not yet quite faced in our time.

In the next few verses, St Paul, as so often, comes from the treatment of a sordid or a trivial matter to the enunciation of a great principle. He points out how ill it becomes the Corinthians to be self-satisfied when this kind of infection is in their body. He points out that since the new Passover has been offered in the person of Christ Himself, we have been purged of these things. We who observe the festival of Christ's Passover must not hark back to the old dispensation; we must look forward to the new dispensation, signified by the unleavened bread, which is sincerity and truth. And so he brings our thoughts away from considering the depths of corruption to the contemplation of the new life of the Gospel.

$6^{12-20}$. This is about prostitution, consorting with harlots. We are of course quite sure that this is wrong, but here we have a discussion about it, and Paul's reasons for saying it is wrong. And in our time I think we have to know why it is wrong. It is not so self-evident to many of our generation as it was in the past. So let us see what Paul had to say about it. He gives four reasons why it is impossible for Christians to be promiscuous.

First, he imagines the supporters of promiscuity as saying that a Christian is free to do anything—he is free of the law, he is not bound down by regulations and prohibitions (or 'inhibitions', as perhaps nowadays we should prefer to say). He is free. Yes, says Paul, he is free, but he will in fact do only that which is profitable to the Christian life. Freedom does not mean that you will do everything that is within your power. Freedom means that you will do that which is profitable to your salvation and profitable to others, that which builds up and does not destroy. That's his first reason. It concerns the people called 'antinomians', who think that once you are a Christian, you are not bound by the moral law. You will know that one of John Wesley's biggest controversies was with people who spoke in these terms, perhaps about this particular matter and no doubt about many others.

In giving his second reason, he imagines once again that the supporters of promiscuity are speaking. They insist, he says, that sexual intercourse is just a natural function of the body, like eating and drinking, with no spiritual significance, a matter of the body only. Now there are many people who say that today. I can remember that in my youth Bertrand Russell was saying that sexual intercourse is just like having a glass of water—as natural as that, and as unimportant as that. Whether he still says that I don't know, but he certainly said it in those days, and he believed it in those days, and his views have always carried weight in this respect; they have certainly been echoed and put into practice in our time. Paul answers by agreeing that eating and drinking are just natural functions and in due course they will come to an end. Just as there will be no sermons in heaven, there will be no banquets or midnight feasts or picnics; eating and drinking belong to this world. They are none the worse for that, but they belong to this world and not the next. The Kingdom of God is not eating and drinking. But sexual intercourse is a different matter. It is not to be equated with eating and drinking as a natural function of the body. It is different because it involves the 'body'. What Paul says about this is not at once clear to us, because of the ambiguity in the use of the word 'body'. When we read the word 'body', we think it just applies to the flesh. Paul means the whole personality by the word 'body'. Please don't forget that. Sexual intercourse, he says, involves the 'body', that is, the whole personality, and the 'body' in the sense of the whole personality survives death to take part in the resurrection. I would suggest to you that this is a very, very important truth about sexual relations. You cannot regard sex as a purely bodily function; it involves everything, and therefore, of course, the argument in support of promiscuity breaks down.

The third point is that we who belong to Christ are linked with Christ in His body; how can we possibly link our bodies with a harlot's? If we are totally committed to Christ and united with Him, it is surely a sheer impossibility that we shall at the next opportunity link our personalities with harlots. It's a terrible denial of our whole religion to do anything of that sort.

The fourth point is that our bodies, our whole personalities, are temples of God's Holy Spirit. They belong to Him, not to us; we have made them over to Him. They have been bought at a price, the precious blood of Jesus Christ. They don't belong to us any more. Therefore, we must honour God with them, and we dare not do anything which dishonours Him, or makes them over to someone else.

$7^{1-7}$. What is Paul saying here about marriage? I think he means, in one sentence, that it is perfectly all right for those who have not the special gift of continence. In other words, Paul thinks that just as the Holy Spirit gives to people the special gift, the *charisma*, of prophetic preaching, or of speaking with tongues, so He also gives to some the special gift of continence. It's a very good thing to have it (Paul himself obviously claims to have it), but if you haven't got that gift, and after all it is not your fault that you haven't got it, it's no kind of discredit to you. If you haven't got that gift it is a good thing to be married. Within marriage, if that is your lot, you are not to pretend that you are not married; you are not to indulge in—or rather, 'indulge' is not the word—, you are not to hold yourself down to an unnatural abstinence. The husband must give the wife what is due to her, and the wife must give the husband what is due to him. 'Do not deny yourselves to one another, except when you agree upon a temporary abstinence in order to devote yourselves to prayer.'

I think you should notice that even in this, which I am bound to call a grudging approval of marriage, Paul does assert the equality of husband and wife. The husband must give the wife her due, and the wife must give the husband his due. The wife cannot claim her body as her own, it is her husband's; and the husband cannot claim his body as his own, it is his wife's. When he says in verse 6, 'All this I say by way of concession, not command', I think he means that he hasn't got a universal law to make for everybody. He is making allowances for different situations in which different people are. He is not going to say you must not be married, and he is not going to say you must be married. Each man must act according to the gift which the Holy Spirit has given to him.

$7^{8-9}$. 'Better be married than burn with vain desire'. This advice after all is realistic! It was only the prudery of our Victorian forefathers that made people think that this was a silly thing for Paul to say. Once again he is on his point that continence is a special gift. It's a good thing to have that gift, but if people haven't got it, they should look round for someone to marry. It is not, if I may say so, an instruction to get married as soon as you are engaged—that's not the point at all. The point is that a life of continence is too difficult for some people to sustain.

**7¹⁰⁻¹¹.** 'Now this time', Paul says, 'it's a ruling which is not mine, but the Lord's; a wife must not separate herself from her husband. If she does she must either remain unmarried or be reconciled to her husband; and a husband must not divorce his wife.' Here he is referring back to the prohibition of divorce which we find in the Gospels. He says divorce is not allowable for Christians; it is forbidden by the Lord. You may want to discuss that, but that is what he says here. If it does happen in spite of this prohibition, there must be no remarriage while the other partner is alive.

**7¹²⁻¹⁶.** This brings us to a very particular and common problem in Paul's time, that of a Christian who is married to a heathen. I imagine that many such Christians said, 'Well, this is fine, this gives me a chance to get rid of him, and I can now divorce him with a good conscience.' On a higher level they may have said, 'This husband of mine is not in sympathy with my ideas, my new ideas, and I am surely at liberty to free myself from him.' To the supporters of this view the answer is, 'No; if the heathen partner is willing to remain in the bonds of matrimony with his Christian partner then divorce is not to be thought of'—and for a very good reason, you will notice. Here is what you might call Christian optimisim; the Christian may convert his heathen partner, and to give up the hope of converting your heathen partner by divorcing him or her is indeed to show lack of faith in Christ. Think of it—as a wife you may be your husband's salvation, or as a husband you may be your wife's salvation.

He goes farther still in verse 14, for he says that the heathen husband now belongs to God through his Christian wife, and the heathen wife belongs to God through her Christian husband; otherwise their children would not belong to God, whereas in fact they do. We have here a sense of the solidarity of the family which we in our time have largely lost. Paul is even prepared to say that if one member of the family, or at any rate one of the married pair, is Christian, then there is a sense in which the other partner is taken up into the Christian faith. Now that requires for us a certain amount of swallowing, but it does in fact point to the idea of the family as an unbreakable unity, which you will find in the early documents of Christianity, and which we ought not to despise. The notion of the solidarity of the Christian family extends to the question of children. We find it a little difficult sometimes to believe that children should be baptized. But Paul, I am sure, would have no difficulty about it at all. It is fairly clear, as a matter of fact, if you look at all the evidence, that in early Christian times the children of Christian parents were in fact baptized, and this fits in entirely with this notion of the solidarity of the family. If the father or the mother belongs to Christ, he or she brings the whole family in with him; and that is borne out by the second part of verse 14: 'Otherwise your children would not belong to God, whereas in fact they do.' And, in the same way, so does the heathen husband. No one would deny that this passage has a relevance to our own time.

$7^{17-24}$. This raises the question of slavery. The general principle that Paul is enunciating here is that you should remain in the condition of life in which you were when you became a Christian. If you were a slave, you should make no tremendous efforts to become free. You should take a chance of freedom if it offers itself, in any reasonable way, but you should not kick against slavery, you should not rebel against your condition. You should be willing to be a slave as a Christian if you were a slave before you were a Christian. That is a hard doctrine for us. It's a specially hard doctrine, I would think, for the under-privileged and suppressed nations of the earth. I suggest that we have got to re-think it in terms of modern conditions. If I may offer you a hint as to the re-thinking, this passage does not include a prohibition against the proper emancipation of subject nations; the prohibition which we here have is against the individual himself taking the law into his own hands. I don't think Paul is dealing with the larger problem of the emancipation of slaves as a whole, or of subject nations as a whole. He is telling the individual person not to take matters into his own hands and murder his master, or use some other violent means of making himself free.

$7^{25-35}$. Paul is here giving advice as to whether people should change their state, and in particular whether people who are not married should get married. The whole of this passage, of course, is dominated by the thought of the imminence of the Lord's coming. Because the Lord's coming is imminent, every Christian lives in a state of stress. He is, as it were, all packed up for a journey, and simply waiting for the bus to arrive. It may come at any moment, and therefore he must not take his attention away from central things; he must not, like the foolish virgins in the parable, look aside to other matters and fill in his time by distractions. He must have his mind concentrated on the imminence of the Lord's coming, in case when He comes he should be found absent. That is the dominating thought of this passage, and I think we have to understand that before we can understand the rest.

'In view of this', he says to us, 'if you are unmarried, the best thing for you to do is to remain unmarried, and if you have been divorced, don't look around for your wife's successor. Remain as you are because the end is near. You must take your mind off this world, and fix your mind on the coming of the Lord; and that being so, that being the atmosphere in which we live, you can see the obvious advantage of being unmarried. A married man must look after his family, he is bound to have his attention occupied by these things; a married woman must look after her family, her mind is full of all sorts of things; whereas if you are not married you can concentrate on the Lord's business.' I can't help feeling that Paul would have been a little nearer to reality, if he had not said that the unmarried or celibate woman cares for the Lord's business, but rather that the unmarried or celibate woman *has the opportunity of* caring for the Lord's business. He is a little optimistic about the subject of unmarried women's conversations. But possibly, if we had that sense of urgency in which the Church lived in his own time, matters would be different.

$7^{36-8}$. These are the strangest verses perhaps in the whole strange chapter. I don't think you will know any parallel in modern life to the situation here described, and I think we should just look at it and pass on. It was a practice in the early Church, and one which became quite common after Paul's, time, to have what were called 'spiritual brides'. That is to say, a man and a woman would live together in spiritual partnership, with the strict vow to have no kind of physical contact. It was thought to be a very meritorious exercise in self-control. You can see, of course, the abuses to which it was liable, and I rather think that Paul is not entirely in favour of it, but as usual he does not actually forbid it. What he does say (sensible advice surely) is that if you can manage it, if you have the gift for such continence, the relationship is no doubt satisfactory, but if not, then the best thing you can do is to marry. And the wish to marry is not a disgrace, it is a recognition of your calling in the Lord. That is what I think this is all about. It's been a much disputed passage and there are other interpretations of it, but the general body of scholars are now agreed on the explanation which I have just given you.

$7^{39-40}$. A widow is not forbidden to remarry (as is obvious from the annals of Christian history), but in view of the urgency of the times she will do better not to do so. But Paul doesn't insist upon it, although he claims that the Spirit of God guides him in the advice which he gives.


These are the remarks about the relation between men and women that Paul makes in this letter, and we must ask whether they add up to a positive doctrine of Christian sexual ethics for today. Today, quite obviously, what we need is a positive doctrine.

Paul is very greatly influenced by the imminence of Christ's return to earth, and that immediately makes it hard for us to get directly into his mind. We cannot seriously live with the thought that the Lord may return at any day, although indeed He may. We can't go on living under that pressure as the early Christians did. But that does not mean that we ought to be exempt from the real urgency of the Gospel. We are not to live as those who have all time at our disposal. Running through the whole of the New Testament there is the recurrent note that time is short, and it has been repeated as you know in many secular statements today. Sir Charles Snow for instance is quoted as saying: 'We haven't much time.' A Christian is bound to agree. But it's very hard to resist the suspicion, which must come in to your minds as you read these passages, that Paul has, niggling away in the bottom of his conscience, a thought that sex is in itself an evil and undesirable thing. And if so, Paul is running contrary to the main message of the Bible, which has no objection to sex as such at all. It is very important to be clear about this ourselves. The Bible as a whole rejoices in the gift of sex, as one of God's good gifts, and if Paul is tainted with some kind of oriental asceticism, which comes in from some other source that we cannot trace, he is contradicting the Gospels and the Old Testament. That should be said quite plainly and definitely. We may rather suspect of him of this, and if we conclude that our suspicion is justified, we are saying that he is against the general run of biblical teaching.

But fortunately what he says here is not all he has to say about sex, and he is not to be judged by this passage alone. There is a more mature handling of the matter by him in the Epistle to the Ephesians,[1] and I now direct your attention to Ephesians, Chapter 5 verse 21 onwards:—

' Be subject to one another out of reverence for Christ.

' Wives, be subject to your husbands as to the Lord; for the man is the head of the woman, just as Christ also is the head of the church. Christ is, indeed, the Saviour of the

---

[1] This Epistle may not be from the hand of St Paul himself, but it certainly comes from St Paul's circle.

body; but just as the church is subject to Christ, so must women be to their husbands in everything.

' Husbands, love your wives, as Christ also loved the church and gave himself up for it, to consecrate it, cleansing it by water and word, so that he might present the church to himself all glorious, with no stain or wrinkle or anything of the sort, but holy and without blemish. In the same way men also are bound to love their wives, as they love their own bodies. In loving his wife a man loves himself. For no one ever hated his own body: on the contrary, he provides and cares for it; and that is how Christ treats the church, because it is his body, of which we are living parts. Thus it is that (in the words of Scripture) " a man shall leave his father and mother and shall be joined to his wife, and the two shall become a single body ". It is a great truth that is hidden here. I for my part refer it to Christ and to the church, but it applies also individually: each of you must love his wife as his very self; and the woman must see to it that she pays her husband all respect.'

Now please do not be unduly diverted by the emphasis in the first verses on the obedience of the wife to the husband. That is there, of course, but the passage also contains the beginning of a very great and creative idea, the full extent of which we have not ourselves yet realized. Here, surely, we have the beginnings of the idea that in marriage there is the union of two whole personalities, who treat each other as such and respect each other as such, two whole persons on an equality with each other, bound to each other by mutual respect and loyalty and love, a relationship beginning no doubt with a physical bond but extending into every part of human life. This surely represents Paul's most mature thought. So my advice to you about the passage in 1 Corinthians is to treat it with respect and understanding, and to combine it with what Paul says in the Epistle to the Ephesians; or better still, as I would suggest, take the view expressed in Ephesians as Paul's real view and accept as much of 1 Corinthians as we find to be truly consistent with what he says in the Epistle to the Ephesians. In other words bring the two things together, and prefer Ephesians!

I am now going to do what I haven't done on the other passages we have discussed, and that is, add my own comments on the subject in hand. We in our time are faced with three main views of sex.

First of all, there is ' the contemporary view ', if I may call it such, and I don't think I parody it when I say that many of our contemporaries think that the relationship between man and woman boils down in the end always to physical union. That's all there is, in the end, to it, whatever else we may say about it. People who hold this view will say that there is no objection to this fact; you may take as much sexual intercourse and pleasure as you fancy; to abstain from it is probably a sign of non-virility, and to object to it, to hold up your hands in horror, is to show that you have inhibitions and guilt complexes. These people are not absolutely against marriage. ' If you find that you have something in common with a woman or man other than sexual or physical attraction and there is some prospect of making a go of it, well, get married ', they say. ' Marriage has economic advantages, it gives the man a home, it gives the woman a protector, and so on. But, of course, if marriage does not work out that way it can be ended as easily as it is begun '. That, I think, is a fairly strongly and widely held view.

The second view with which we are faced, but not of course so vividly these days, is Paul's ' Corinthian ' view, if I may put it so. ' Sexual relations outside marriage are wrong because sexual relations involve the union of two whole personalities, and that is something that is only possible and proper in marriage. In marriage man is the ruling partner, the woman must be subject to him; but the man must be reasonable and fair in the exercise of his control. He remains the master; he is a just master, a considerate master, a charitable master, but master '. Now that is the second view.

I put it to you that both these views are in a way a degradation of woman. In the first view, the degradation of woman is involved because, as far as I know, the sexual relation is for the woman, at least at first, much more than a physical union. Much more than the mere physical body is involved, and therefore of course casual sexual relationships have a different effect on a woman from what they have on a man. Secondly, the woman is normally left to deal with the consequences of such relationships. I don't mean only the consequences in the form of a child (in our day she is often able to avoid or deal with that kind of consequence); I mean also the emotional and deeply personal consequences. And, thirdly, this view leads to the degradation of a woman because, when sex is made trivial, just a matter of thrills and excitements, men very quickly come to think of women as playthings, and the words 'play' and 'things' are both important in that joint word. I thought that came out very clearly in a TV tribute to the late Ernest Hemingway. Hemingway was by general consent a great writer, and he was a great prophet of the modern conception of sex. He was also an *embodiment* of that particular principle of life, and the woman in the TV tribute said that the trouble about Hemingway was that he regarded women simply as means for his own pleasure. She didn't put it quite like that, but that is what it came to—and that is what happens when this notion of sex prevails. You see it in ancient Rome, you see it in the Restoration period in England, and you see it I think in twentieth-century Western civilization. I believe, however, that in a much more subtle way and a much more dignified way the 'Corinthian' view of Paul also leads in the same direction. The dominance of man over woman really limits the woman to certain departments of life, certain chores; and, since a man has within himself undoubtedly the desire to dominate, and as now he has from St Paul liberty to dominate, he does dominate, and tends to deny the woman the right to develop her own individuality and to do those things, apart from child-rearing and housewifery, of which she is capable. This is another and more refined form of the degradation of woman.

The third view is the one suggested by Paul in the Epistle to the Ephesians—the self-committal of two persons to each other, beginning, probably, as a matter of physical attraction, but extending to every part of life and every realm of life, so that the two people, bound in marriage, working together, praying together, and serving together, are whole-life partners. There is no doubt in my mind that this is the Christian view, though we have not yet worked it out in practice or in theory; and if it is the Christian view, it seems to me to give a clue to all relations between men and women. I think one can judge the suggestions that are made about sexual behaviour, the experiments that we may be asked to try to put up with, by one simple law. Does that which is suggested serve the Christian idea of marriage? Does it fit in, or does it not? If it does, even if it is against ancient conventions, we should approve it. But if it is going to militate against the proper understanding and fulfilment of Christian marriage, then we must be against it. This is a very simple criterion, which can be applied to a great number of the things that are suggested to us in all sorts of ways today. We are not to be ruled by convention, ancient or modern; we are to be guided rather by the notion of Christian marriage as the life-long and whole-life union of two whole personalities in Jesus Christ, and do everything to promote it, and nothing to hinder it.

STUDY FIVE

## THE CHRISTIAN AND HIS BRETHREN IN HEATHEN SOCIETY
(1 Corinthians $6^{1-11}$, $8^{1-13}$, $9^{1-27}$, $10^{1-33}$)

$6^{1-11}$. Paul is shocked to hear that some of the Corinthians even went to the length of suing their fellow-Christians in the city law courts; that meant that a Christian was to be found citing a fellow-Christian, and that the case was to be heard by pagans. In such a case as this, Paul has no difficulty in showing that they ought to put up with injustice rather than go to law. And if there were matters that needed to be straightened out, surely, he says, there was a wise Christian available to do what was necessary. In other words, he laid it upon the Corinthians not to go to law with one another under any conditions; it was much better to be unjustly treated than to go before a pagan law court, much better indeed to be unjustly treated than to go before a law court at all.

This prohibition of going to law comes rather harshly on our ears, and few of us, however Christian we are, are willing to admit the rightness of Paul's prohibition of seeking justice when our interests are damaged. Moreover, since the laws in all modern countries, in all modern Western countries at any rate, are so greatly influenced by long traditions of Christian thought and practice, the situation is very different from what it was in Corinth, and most of us are quite clear that we need not hesitate to bring matters to court.

It is certainly true that Paul was dealing with a situation quite different from our own. But two things from what he says still apply. In countries where the law courts are not held according to the tradition of law built up under the influence of Christianity, the justice administered may indeed be something other than what Christians may expect. For instance, in East Germany and other Communist countries, there is no guarantee that the principles of justice are the same as we should find in countries where Christian democracy flourishes. And it might well be true that in such countries Christians should at all costs avoid bringing law suits, especially against their fellow-Christians; for to do so would be to connive at injustice.

The other relevant advice is that litigiousness in any country, eastern or western, is always to be avoided. Some of the most disgraceful things in the history of the Christian Church have happened when Christians have sought to maintain their rights against other Christians by bringing actions in the courts. When questions of property have arisen between Christians who have disagreed with each other, and the judges have been asked to look into them; or when, in order to maintain a position within the Church, a man or group has appealed to the law courts, and the courts have pronounced the action of ecclesiastical authority illegal, Christians have not shown to the world a good advertisement of Christian love and forbearance. And, in general, surely it is true that when Christians disagree with each other, as even Christians may about the possession of property, or about the validity of agreements and so on, it is a matter, if at all possible, to be settled between them, perhaps by the advice of a wise Christian or group of Christians. So a part of St Paul's teaching which appears to be very much out-of-date is not perhaps quite as out-of-date as it seems.

**8, 9, 10.** There is one dominant theme throughout these chapters, but a number of subordinate themes keep on intruding, and one of the subordinate themes sometimes takes up the whole of St Paul's attention for several verses, so that it is easy to lose the thread of the discourse, and hard to keep our minds on the main subject. We most of us have that difficulty when listening to certain sermons and lectures, and so perhaps we can cope with it when it occurs in Paul's letters!

Paul has a certain situation in mind about which he has been consulted by the Corinthians in their letter. The situation is this. The city of Corinth was as full of pagan temples of all sorts as an English town is full of public houses. These temples were used for various kinds of worship. Some were shrines of the Greek gods of ancient times, others were for cults which had been recently imported from the Middle East. One of the common customs in temples of all sorts was that of holding sacramental meals in honour of the god or goddess to whom the temple was dedicated. The god or goddess who was honoured by the meal was thought to be present; and the worshippers when they took this meal together believed that they shared in the life of the deity, and received into themselves the power and vitality that belongs to him or her. That was part of the regular religious life of Corinth. Temples were also used for more informal purposes. A group of people, let us say a social club or a family celebrating an anniversary, might book a temple for the afternoon and evening. As they had hired the temple for the occasion only, they had no official connexion with the god or goddess involved. The temple was just a convenient place for them to dine in, just as you might hire a church hall for a wedding. The god or goddess might sometimes be the president or patron of the society. There was a society in Oxford in the thirties called the Shakespeare Society. It would meet for dinner once a month, and the president, beginning the proceedings, would announce that he was about to read the Bard. But, before he could start, a member of the society would propose that the Bard be regarded as having been read; this was immediately seconded, put to the vote, and carried; the copy of Shakespeare was put away and the real business of the evening began, eating the dinner and drinking the wine. In something of the same sort of way in a Corinthian temple the deity was the official patron of the gathering, but the real purpose of the gathering was not religious at all. Now these uses of temples presented a problem for Christians. Should they eat in the idol temple or not? Were they condoning idol worship if they did? Were they indeed participating in idol worship if they ate at a sacramental meal or a social meal under the auspices of the heathen god?

But that was not the only difficulty; there was a more humdrum one as well. All the meat in the butchers' shops in Corinth could very well have come from one of the temples. The temple-worshippers brought their animals to be sacrificed to the god. The priest on duty killed the animals, kept some of the meat for the god—usually the part of the animal which was not easily digestible by human stomachs—kept some for himself which he would use for his own cuisine, and sold the rest to the butcher. This was a perfectly natural and legitimate arrangement, because priests did not receive a salary, and it was well understood that the meat was a perquisite of the priest; the money which he obtained from selling the meat to the butchers was his own. This meant that the butchers' shops were full of meat which had been sacrificed to idols. If you went to the butcher to buy meat, you could never be sure whether or not you were buying meat which had been offered to an idol; there was no special label on the meat which had been so offered. Should the Christians buy meat in the shops, or should they avoid meat altogether?

Even that was not all. Christians might well be invited out to supper by a pagan friend. Ought they to refuse to eat meat under such conditions?—for they could scarcely ask whether the meat on the table had been offered in a pagan temple (in the first place their host would not know; in the second place it was not a very polite question). That is the situation. Paul's answer to these various problems is in these chapters.

**8.** Some of the Christians in Corinth had pointed out quite rightly that pagan deities had no real existence at all, and that therefore the meat offered to them was in no way different from any other meat. They therefore asserted their right to eat any meat that was offered to them in the shops; and also their right to attend social occasions in pagan temples whenever they felt inclined. When the local glee club, or the Corinthian Legion, or whatever it was, met for the annual dinner in the pagan temple, they saw no reason why they should not go.

Paul in this chapter admits the truth of their theological

argument; he admits that of course the gods to whom the temples are dedicated have no real existence. But he comments on the arrogance of the people who made claims of this sort. They were, of course, in their own opinion, enlightened people, people who were superior to the scruples and superstitions and prejudices of others (we are familiar with such people); they are probably the same as those who are mentioned in other parts of the Epistle as boasting superior spiritual knowledge in other things as well. Having commented on their arrogance, he goes on to show them that there were many Christians, other than themselves, who had an uneasy conscience about anything to do with idol worship; they might not really believe in the idols, but they had an uncomfortable feeling that there might be something in it after all—just as some people in enlightened Western civilizations refuse to go under a ladder, or to do certain things on the thirteenth of the month or on a Friday. They do not believe that these practices are really dangerous, but they have an uneasy feeling that there might be something in it; better therefore to be on the safe side. Because there are Christians who feel like that, says Paul, however enlightened a man may be, he ought to refrain from anything that may trouble the conscience of another. It is all right for him; he is enlightened and free, but the other man's peace of mind is shaken and his Christian life may be ruined. Therefore these enlightened people ought to be ready to show their enlightenment by Christian charity, by refraining from taking part in meals in idol temples, and from buying meat in the butcher's shop, even at the cost of becoming a vegetarian.

**9.** Paul goes on to illustrate the point which he has just made, the point that a Christian ought never to stand on his right to freedom at the cost of hurting others. He illustrates the point by his own case. He shows that he has many rights as an apostle—for instance, the right to be maintained by the Church. For he is clear that it is the duty of the Church to maintain, with food and money and shelter, those who teach and preach. He has also the right, he says, to take a wife round with him on his travels, and to say that she also should be a charge upon the Church. He has these rights and others; but he does not exercise them. When he has said this, his mind goes on (we might even say, wanders) to many other aspects of his apostolic task, and he feels himself immediately impelled to say: 'Of *course* I do not claim my rights, of *course* I do not claim any credit for preaching the gospel; that was a charge laid upon me. It gives me a deep satisfaction; in fact it would be misery *not* to preach the gospel. I have become all things to all men, in order at all costs to win some for Jesus Christ.'

Then he returns to the point that he is making, and goes on to warn those who think themselves strong in faith and character not to despise the power of temptation. The Christian life for them, as it is for everyone, is a continuous course of training in self-mastery. It is all very well for them to claim to be free from weaknesses; they had better be very careful about it, for every Christian must keep himself in continual training; he must prepare at least as much as any athlete in training for the Games, by keeping his body in subjection, by accepting limitation in food and drink, and by refusing to exercise the rights which may be his, but which for his own sake and others ought not to be asserted.

**9⁵.** ' Have I no right to take a Christian wife about with me ? '

As far as we know he had no wife, and so perhaps this example is a somewhat abstract one! People have supposed that Paul was married or a widower, on the ground that Rabbis and members of the Sanhedrin had to be married. But there is no good ground for thinking he was either of these things. And what he has to say on marriage and the relations of men and women in earlier chapters makes it very clear, surely, that he has no direct experience of married life.

**9⁹.** ' " A threshing ox shall not be muzzled." Do you suppose God's concern is with oxen ? Or is the reference clearly to ourselves ? '

Paul quotes a passage from the Law containing a very humane instruction. But he is not willing to take this instruction literally. He simply cannot think that God is interested in the welfare of animals, and he suggests that it must be an allegorical reference to preachers of the Gospel. It is a sidelight on Paul's faith (and indeed on the faith of Jews and early Christians alike), when we find that he does not think that God has any interest in the welfare of oxen. The Bible is certainly not full of references to the welfare of animals; it would be difficult to find a text or charter for the Royal Society for the Prevention of Cruelty to Animals anywhere in the Bible, except perhaps in the last words of the Book of Jonah.

9²⁴. 'You know (do you not?) that at the sports all the runners run the race, though only one wins the prize. Like them run to win.'
The analogy to the Christian life is not at all perfect here, because in the games—Paul has especially in mind the Isthmian games, which were regularly held in the neighbourhood of Corinth—, as he rightly says, only one man comes first in any given race. The analogy would only be complete if in the Christian life only one, only the Christian who does better than anybody else in Christian character, were rewarded, whereas the situation is much more like that which is described in *Alice in Wonderland*, where we are told that everyone has won, and everyone receives prizes. All those who train themselves to the Christian life train themselves to do God's will, receive praise from God. So the analogy does not really work. We do not associate Paul with great interest in athletics, and it is sometimes pointed out that when he uses an analogy from athletics he does not show a perfect knowledge of the principles and technique of the sport which he is describing. But we can at least draw the conclusion that he was not opposed to sport or the exercise of the body. And the awkwardness of the analogy does not blunt the edge of his insistence on self-discipline.

10¹⁻¹⁴. Paul is here still continuing at some length the point which he made at the end of Chapter 9 about the power of temptation, of which even the most advanced and enlightened Christians need to beware. He reminds his readers of the terrible failures of the Israelites: they had received a divine mission, and were indeed engaged in carrying out that mission, and had at that very time turned to idolatry and fornication. The chapter ends by encouraging those who feel weak in the face of temptation. He shows that God will always see to it that we are not tempted beyond our strength to resist. That is sometimes, in the midst of temptation, hard to believe. At such times there is nothing to do but trust in God and rely on His mercy, and seize His help when it comes.

**10¹¹ᵃ.** 'All these things that happened to them were symbolic, and were recorded for our benefit as a warning.'

That probably does not mean that the events described in the Old Testament did not actually happen, and that what we have is an allegorical description. He means rather that they did in fact happen, but that they happened not just as plain events; they happened in order to make clear to us God's purpose, and to be useful to us in our time as a warning.

**10¹¹ᵇ.** 'For upon us the fulfilment of the ages has come'.

Rather a casual reference in the middle of a discussion about something else to a tremendous truth of the Gospel! This is a phrase containing in itself a great deal of the Christian Gospel in miniature. Fulfilment of the ages, Paul says, has come upon us in our day. For Christ is the fulfilment of all the hopes of men. What was promised in the history of ancient Israel and recorded for our benefit by the prophets and historians has all now come true. Most people seem to think that the fulfilment of God's purpose is in the future. I wonder if it is? Christ has come, and with Him the fulfilment intended by God. We live in the epoch which His coming inaugurated; we live in the epoch of His kingdom, the kingdom which has resisted and repelled all sorts of attack, the kingdom which triumphed on the Cross. There Christ defeated all the forces of evil and made His victory secure. Everything that has happened since then is a working out of His victory. Yet there is a further fulfilment still to come, in the consummation of all the ages, when all men, including those who deny Him now, will recognize the sovereignty of God.

**10¹⁵⁻³³.** Now Paul comes back to the particular subject which he is supposed to be discussing. He makes special reference to the question of attending religious meals in a heathen temple, intended to give communion with the god. Here he shows that sacrifices made to idols are really made to demons, and that to share a sacramental meal in their honour is to hold communion with demonic forces. At this point Paul's way of thinking is less to our liking than at any other time in the Epistle. We sometimes talk about demonic forces, but we hardly believe them to be independent of ourselves. Paul certainly believed that the air which we breathe is peopled by demons, by what he calls 'principalities and powers', under the discipline and control of the 'prince of the power of the air'. He is saying here: 'The idols you worship in the heathen temples are actually demons; for the demons have taken over their temples, and the worship which is claimed for idols is in fact received by demons. The communion which is thought to be with idols is really communion with demons'. This is a view that we find hard to share, but there is good authority for saying that in certain parts of England black magic is done and black masses are celebrated, and it is certain that the belief in demons is still very vigorous in many parts of Africa even where Christianity is accepted, and many Christians continue to hold it. So we must be careful not to dismiss it too lightly.

Paul's main point, of course, is that we cannot mix this ' communion with demons ' with the Christian's communion with Christ, and as he makes it he drops some very valuable hints on the subject of this communion with Christ which is ours in Holy Communion. To drink the wine and eat the bread at the Lord's Supper is to share in the ' blood of Christ ' and the ' body of Christ '. The ' blood of Christ ' surely means ' the death of Christ ' and ' the body of Christ ' means 'the Church of Christ'. Thus at His Supper we share in the benefits of His death, and we become members of His Church. The second point, says Paul, is indicated by the fact that we eat of one loaf at the Supper; by eating one loaf we become one body—on the principle of the old adage, ' We become what we eat.' It will be worth remembering this when we come to Paul's full treatment of the Eucharist in Chapter 11.

Now Paul is able, from $10^{25}$ onwards, to give practical rules for the problem under discussion. Meat on sale in the shops is to be bought without hesitation. Invitations to the homes of pagans are to be accepted, and the food provided is to be eaten, unless it is expressly stated that the meat was offered in an idol's temple; in that case, no Christian will eat it, in order not to harm the consciences and disturb the scruples of his weaker brothers. Paul regards this last as so important that he ends his treatment of the whole matter by stressing it again: we ought to respect the consciences of others, even if it interferes with our own freedom.

The whole discussion may not seem to touch us very nearly.

We certainly do not have exactly the same problems as the early Christians, if we live in officially Christian countries. But our fellow-Christians in Asia and Africa are by no means free from this kind of problem in relation to the established customs of their country, which are heathen through and through. And all of us have to decide our attitude to people in our society whose customs and attitudes are different from ours, and often virtually pagan.

Some of these customs and attitudes we at once repudiate: the restless desire for wealth and power, sexual laxity, the principle of gambling as a way of making money, the love of material comforts, and so on. On grounds of conscience, we refuse to take part in the ' rat race ' which is going on all around us, even if it means that we do not have so large an income or so high a position as we might otherwise be able to get. So far our path is clear.

But other things are not so clear. Our un-Christian friends see nothing wrong in drinking and smoking; they are a pleasant relaxation. Should we cut ourselves off from them because they do these things ? Or should we conform to their ways of doing things on the grounds of our Christian freedom ? Or is there some way in which we can maintain our friendship with non-Christians and our principles at the same time ? On such dilemmas Paul has much to say of help. We must indeed treasure our freedom, but treasure even more our concern for those who have more scruples than ourselves. We must not exercise our freedom to be friendly with those who do not share our views to the extent of causing pangs of conscience to others. And as we exercise our freedom we must beware of temptations, which can come to us however enlightened we are, temptations which come to us in particularly subtle forms, so that it seems simply that we are taking part in some harmless activity when we are in fact being unconsciously drawn into a way of life with which we should have nothing to do. Then again, there are all sorts of things we have a perfect right to do, but to assert all our rights is in fact a form of pride, not an exercise of Christian freedom.

We may notice also the resolve of Paul ' to be all things to all men ', that he may win some for Christ. This is of great relevance to our situation. It may be that somewhere within it lies the key to ' the problem of communication ' about which we talk so much. Paul is suggesting that our real chance of bringing God's message home to our generation is to identify ourselves with our contemporaries, with their hopes and fears, with their aspirations for a better society and their disappointment that it is so long in coming, with their insight, their undoubted insight, into human nature and human motivation, and with their vastly increased understanding of themselves and of society. May it not be that we should identify ourselves with our contemporaries to the utmost limit that we can reach without being affected by that which poisons the life of our society, by the desperation which is sweeping over all classes, by the sensuality to which they fly as their only hope of personal fulfilment? This kind of self-identification with our contemporaries, this being involved in the affairs of our time, this suffering with those who suffer, this working constructively with those who aim at something better for the world, as they strive for the care of the underprivileged, for the prevention of war and injustice, for the development of under-nourished peoples—all this we shall undertake as those whose hope is not in this world only, but in the Lord of all time and of eternity, sovereign of the whole universe. By this identification, and not by passing into a ghetto and simply enjoying our own cosy Christian fellowship and worship, it may be that we shall come to find the key to the problem which defeats us, the problem of putting the Gospel to our society, at last, in the language which it understands.

STUDY SIX

# WORSHIP AND RESURRECTION
(1 Corinthians 11$^{1-34}$, 14$^{1-40}$, 15$^{1-58}$)

**11$^{1-16}$.** 'Should a woman pray bare-headed?' This is one of the situations where Paul does not free himself from the traditions of his past, or from that society which still exists in certain parts of the world today, in which woman is definitely regarded as inferior to man and subordinate to him. But I would point out to you that even here something finer is struggling for expression in Paul's mind. On the question of the relationship between men and women, the emancipation of spirit which belongs to the Christian is probably slower in coming than on any other subject, because of the deep instincts and tangled emotions which are thereby involved. Verse 11 ('woman is as essential to man as man to woman') shows this nobler idea forcing its way to expression. I don't think we have entirely realized the full significance of that yet. So when you feel inclined to deride the other things he says, please remember that he also said that.

Now as to this problem about whether a woman should be veiled in church. We have to distinguish, of course, between the fundamental principles of the Christian religion which come out of St Paul's epistles, and his application of them to circumstances which pass away. And here we surely have the latter, a temporary application of the principles of faith to a situation which has passed away. So I do not suggest for a moment, nor indeed, I gather, does the Archbishop of Canterbury, that women should wear veils whenever they come to church. I think what causes Paul to be particularly conservative on this point is the moral situation in Corinth. It is probably true, although it is not stated, that for a woman not to wear a cover for her head indicated that her reputation was dubious. This situation has to be borne in mind when you read this. With that before us let us look at the actual question at issue.

Paul gives two reasons why a woman should be veiled in church. Firstly, because she has to show respect to man and to God, and that is the proper way to show respect to man and to God in Christian worship. The other reason he gives is that God has indicated that women need their heads to be covered in His presence by giving them an abundance of hair, which is, in the old phrase, their 'crowning glory'. I don't think either of these arguments is very strong and we need not spend very much time over them.

Then in the middle of this passage there is, of course, the most difficult and puzzling verse of all, 11$^{10}$. I can assure you that no one really knows what that means, and we are entitled to have our own opinions about it, but not to lay down the law. 'A sign of authority on her head' most probably means that she must have a sign of the authority which the man exercises over her; it isn't her authority, but the man's. That is borne out by the fact that in Jewish weddings, which are rather different from ours, the bride on the way to the wedding keeps her head uncovered, in token of the freedom which she still possesses, and from the moment of marriage onwards she wears a veil to show that her freedom has now diminished; she is thought thereby to show respect for her husband. This appears to be the kind of point to which Paul is referring here.

The last bit of the verse is more difficult than ever: 'out of regard for the angels.' All kinds of curious speculations have broken out on that subject. The old-fashioned one, which I think we can disregard, is that women should wear a veil on their heads in order to avoid tempting the angels, who may be hovering over the top of the congregation. There is a reference in the Book of Genesis to evil angels who desired the daughters of men, but I don't think this is a thought which comes in here at all; it doesn't really make any sense in this context. It is more likely that Paul gives this instruction, 'out of regard for the angels' because of the *good* angels who are thought to be present in church. St Paul probably did think that when the Christian Church worshipped, the angels and archangels were present, which when you come to think of it is a splendid thought, and in view of their presence, and in view of the presence of God, women should show proper respect by wearing a veil on their heads. I think something of that sort lies behind these rather strange words. I deal with this passage, not because it gives us much of a hint about Christian worship in the present day, but because if people ask questions about it, it is just as well that we should know, if possible, what Paul was getting at. Now we come to a much more serious matter.

11$^{17-34}$. Before we can understand these verses we must call to our mind the picture of worship in the early Church. It was very different from our own, in outer form at any rate. The practice in Corinth was no doubt something like this. The wealthiest member of the Church would throw his home open to Christians for worship on the Lord's Day, and the people would come to this house for worship. There is one kind of worship described in this chapter and another in Chapter 14.

On the occasions described here the people coming to worship would bring with them food and drink, and when they came the food and drink would be pooled, and a distribution would be made to all present. The poorer people who couldn't bring as much as the rich people had as big a share as the rich. That is the original meaning in English, I am told, of a ' picnic '. They came and did this and then took a meal together, a common meal, and after this meal, just as after the Last Supper in Jerusalem, they proceeded to eat the Lord's Supper and take the bread and wine according to the Lord's commandment. This seems to have happened every Sunday and was indeed the central worship of the Church.

You see that it falls into two parts, the eating and drinking of the common meal, and then the eating and drinking of the Lord's Supper. It is customary to call the first part the

'Love Feast'—the '*Agape*'—and this eating of a common meal survived for a certain period into the early Church but was gradually dropped. It has been revived from time to time in the history of the Church, and not least in the early days of the Methodist movement. A very, very simple meal of cake and water was eaten by the Methodists when they met together and then they would proceed from that to spiritual conversation. Sometimes they followed it by the Communion Service, but not always, of course, because they could only do so when an ordained minister was present. The Love Feast in Corinth was, however, always followed by the Lord's Supper.

Now something had gone wrong in Corinth, and Paul's description of it is so vivid that I don't need to repeat it. The rich people had brought better and richer food than the others, and then decided that they would eat it themselves, and some of them had eaten and drunk so much that when it came to the point of eating the Lord's Supper they were not in a fit state to do so.

That can perhaps hardly happen in our worship today! What can hapepn of course is the underlying cause of it, the division between parties in the Church. And therefore, when we read here, 'the result is that when you meet as a congregation, it is impossible for you to eat the Lord's Supper', the words have an unpleasant ring of truth about them. The divisions of the Church of which we are all very conscious really can make it impossible to eat the Lord's Supper, because if we are divided in spirit and in mind it may not be the Lord's Supper that we eat at all. So the basic situation is possible, although the actual form of it doesn't nowadays happen.

In order to bring the point most vividly and properly home to his people, Paul reminds them of what happened on the original occasion of the Lord's Supper. Here we come to a passage which is very familiar to us, I would say *too* familar to us. We ought to look at it again in order that familiarity may not breed neglect. 'The Lord Jesus, on the night of his arrest, took bread and, after giving thanks to God, broke it and said: " This is my body, which is for you; do this as a memorial of me." '

The scholars are still arguing whether the Last Supper was a Passover Feast, or whether it was a special supper of Jesus and His friends which took place on the night before the Passover. The Gospel of St John seems to indicate the latter view, and the three other Gospels seem to indicate that it was a Passover Feast. For a long time it was generally held by the scholars that St John was right, and that it was not a Passover Feast that Jesus shared with His disciples. Most recent books on the subject, however, rather go the other way. My own judgement has changed on this matter and I tend to think that it is fairly certain that it was a Passover meal that Jesus took with His friends.

He and His friends formed together what the ancient Jews called a *Chaburah*, a religious society, rather like the Religious Society which the Methodists formed in the early days inside the Church of England—a society of men who stayed a good deal of their time together with a rabbi as their leader, and who had certain customs and practices of their own which they carried out within the Jewish Church. If the first three Gospels are right, Jesus and His *Chaburah* met together on this the last night of His life for the Passover Supper. The normal thing, of course, was for Jews on this occasion to meet in their families, and the father of the family would preside over the family and all the careful and ancient ritual connected with it. Jesus did not meet with His family, or rather His family was His *Chaburah*. At the start of the meal, after thanksgiving to God, there was a prayer which was always said by the father of the family: ' Blessed art Thou, O Lord our King, King of the world, who broughtest forth bread out of the earth ', and I think we may assume that Jesus, as ' the father of the family ', very probably used that prayer on this occasion. Then he went on to say something that was *not* normally said at a Passover Supper: ' This is my body, which is for you; do this as a memorial of me.'

Now here, you see, is the unique and distinctive feature of the Supper of the Lord. ' This is my body '. Don't for the moment let us worry about the theological controversies which those simple words have called out—Jesus is saying (isn't He?), ' This is I, myself.' (' Body ', you will remember, does not mean simply the flesh, but the whole self) ' Which is for you ' means ' offered for you ', 'sacrificed for you '. Of course, Jesus can't easily be imagined to have meant that the bread had been, as it were, changed into His body, because His body was present with them. He is saying under the symbolism of bread that He Himself is sacrificed on their behalf. ' Do this as a memorial of me.' They are to do it apparently in the future. It is not just once and for all. They are to break the bread when they meet for worship. They cannot have His physical presence with them, but they can go through the actions which He went through on this dark night as a memorial of Him.

The word ' memorial ' sounds as though Jesus is instituting a commemoration to a dead hero, or patron saint, or the founder of a society; but we do grave injustice to this word ' memorial ' if we take it that way. The word that Jesus used means much more than a mere commemoration; it means that when in the years to come they broke the bread and distributed it among themselves, they were bringing back into their midst the very presence of Jesus Christ; they were not just ' remembering ' Him, but almost, we might say, 'calling Him up into their presence', so that He Himself was with them, just as truly (although not as visibly) as He was on the night on which He was betrayed. And that applies to us also. We cannot understand these words without believing in the Real Presence of the Lord at His Supper. He is the Host at every Supper of the Lord. Remember, too, what Paul has said about sharing in the body and blood of Christ in $10^{14-22}$. This does not involve us in a great deal of argument at this point as to what form His presence takes and whether the bread and wine are ' transubstantiated ', and so on. It involves us in the simple and profound faith that He Himself is present among us.

' In the same way, he took the cup after supper, and said: " This cup is the new covenant sealed by my blood. Whenever you drink it, do this as a memorial of me."' He has just spoken of the sacrifice in which He is to offer Himself for the sins of the world. Now He refers to another aspect of his death. ' This cup is the new covenant ', the covenant referred to and promised by Jeremiah (31$^{31}$), the promise of God that He will make a new covenant with His people, a promise now fulfilled. The covenant is sealed with His blood. It is not a bargain, as in the older sense of ' covenant ', but a gift of God by which He forgives us out of His own pure grace and receives us to Himself, though we have no right to be so received. This one-sided covenant we have simply to accept, because God offers it to us out of His free love. ' This cup is the new covenant sealed by my blood. Whenever you drink it, do this as a memorial of me '. That is: ' Do this, and when you do it I myself will be present among you, reminding you of this new covenant and sealing it once again in your hearts '.

That is the meaning, as far as I can see it, or part of the meaning, of the solemn words of Jesus on this solemn occasion. Paul draws the moral: ' For every time you eat this bread and drink the cup, you proclaim the death of the Lord, until he comes '—you proclaim the power of the death of the Lord, you proclaim His sacrifice for the sins of the whole world, you proclaim the covenant which He has sealed with His blood, and you will go on doing it until He comes again in glory and all things are fulfilled and earth is transformed into Heaven.

Thinking and speaking about the Sacrament of the Lord's Supper has become almost the professional preserve of theologians and ministers and priests, and this is wrong. There need be nothing abstruse and complicated about the Lord's Supper for the Lord's people. Of course, it does involve theological questions into which some people are required to enter, but fundamentally it is the fulfilment of the Lord's promise of His presence to His own people, and you don't need to be a theologian to think about that. You certainly don't need to be a theologian to come up to the Lord's Table and receive His Body and Blood. So I would commend to you this passage for deep meditation, and ask you in your own way to pass on your thoughts about it to people whom you meet.

It follows from all this, says Paul, that anybody who eats the bread and drinks the cup of the Lord unworthily will be guilty of desecrating the Body and Blood of the Lord; and therefore we must test ourselves before we eat the bread and drink the cup. The Sacrament is not meant to be taken lightly, or easily; it is a serious and solemn occasion, in which we dare not take part unless we have looked into our hearts. It we do not test ourselves, if we drink unworthily, Paul says, we shall not 'discern the Body'. In the *New English Bible* the word 'Body' is spelt with a capital B, which means of course that it is the Body *of Christ*. We shall not be able to distinguish the Body of Christ from mere bread.

There is a strange verse following this that we must notice: 'That is why many of you are feeble and sick, and a number have died.' Paul seems to hold the view that to take the Lord's Supper unworthily is to bring upon oneself the danger of illness and death. 'If we examined ourselves', he says, 'we should not thus fall under judgement'.

**$14^{1-33}$.** Paul now deals with another matter of Christian worship, here worship of a less formal kind. There is surely in this chapter a courteous disparagement of the gift of speaking with tongues, at any rate in public worship. It is useful, he says, to those who have it, but not of much use to the rest of us. In the verses which follow, his point is: suppose somebody comes in from the Gentile world and hears somebody speaking with tongues; he will think he has come into a madhouse—more especially as it appears to have happened in Corinth that several people spoke with tongues at the same time. He points out that if people speak with tongues, at any rate they should only do so one at a time, and goes on to say with great common sense that if a man speaks with tongues it is important that someone should interpret what he says. 'If you can interpret it yourself, well and good, but if you can't, at least make sure that somebody does.' This is a chapter which is fairly plain to understand, but once again it brings out a very important principle: 'For the God who inspires them is not a God of disorder but of peace' ($14^{33}$). Orderliness is a part of worship. Inspiration is also a part of worship. Orderliness can of course sometimes quench inspiration, but inspiration can sometimes quench orderliness, and the essence of worship is the integration of orderliness and inspiration. This is sufficient answer to those who say: 'You must *either* have extempore worship *or* you must have liturgical worship, and *either* spontaneity *or* dignity.' We are not compelled to choose between these two; rather we should seek a balance of spontaneity and dignity.

$14^{34-5}$. Not only are these verses puzzling in themselves; they also create considerable difficulties when we look at the rest of the epistle. You will not have forgotten the passage about the covering of women's heads in church ($11^5$), in which Paul says: 'A woman, on the contrary, brings shame on her head if she prays or prophesies bare-headed.' The obvious implication of that is that it is perfectly all right for a woman to speak in a service if she prays or prophesies with a veil on her head, and if we had not this passage here we should certainly suppose that that is what St Paul is saying. We also know that in the early Church there were women who prophesied. In Acts, you will remember, there is one man mentioned whom Paul visits, and doesn't as far as we know tell off, who has no fewer than four daughters who were 'prophets' (local preachers?). So that we really have a very considerable difficulty here, and the difficulty is either increased or diminished, according to your point of view, if you remember that in the Greek manuscripts of 1 Corinthians this little paragraph (verses 34 and 35) appears sometimes after verse 33 and sometimes after verse 40—as if the scribe was not quite certain where it came in. When you get that kind of phenomenon in manuscripts you begin to wonder whether the passage in question is part of the original text at all.

After much consideration I am inclined to think that this may not be part of the original letter. You may conclude that I say that because I am a feminist! But I hope I have explained to you the difficulties of taking it as it stands. It is at any rate possible that when somebody read the epistle after St Paul's time, he did not think that Paul had been sufficiently stringent on the matter of women speaking in church, and therefore put a little note in the margin, as to what the practice in the churches was, and this note in the margin became ultimately incorporated into the text. I don't think one often wants to say that about passages in the New Testament, but one might perhaps be entitled to say it now. Otherwise I have not found any very convincing explanations for the contradiction between this passage and 11[5].

One more point about worship. These practices of the early Church don't very much resemble ours. I suppose if you were to make a literal comparison, the meetings of the Quakers are rather more like what is described in Chapter 14 than our own services are, and we have to ask ourselves, quite deliberately, whether the worship of the Church in modern times really corresponds with the worship of the early Church. We should ask that question first of all about the Lord's Supper. I think we can fairly persuade ourselves that what we do at the Lord's Supper is in direct continuity with what happened at the Last Supper. All sorts of elaborations have come into it, and the whole history of the Lord's Supper is very interesting and very revealing, but we can claim to maintain continuity. It is not quite so easy to fit in our other services with what happens in chapter 14. The question which we ought to ask ourselves is one suggested by John Henry Newman. He held that if you looked at the services of the Church in his day you could see what you would see if you looked at the early Church services through a microscope. A microscope shows up all sorts of details which are not visible to the naked eye, and Newman held that if you looked at the early Church's services under a microscope you would see all the developments which have since occurred. He was a trifle optimistic. There are many things about modern worship which are not, I suspect, in accordance with the worship of the early Church. Nevertheless I hope that *in principle* Newman's claim is true. Anyway there is our test. Is our worship in accordance with the spirit of the early Church, or have we brought in things which are not Christian, which are sub-Christian, or which are just convenient to us?

**15.** This is the climax of the epistle, yet in a way it comes in quite casually. St Paul has heard that there are people in Corinth who deny the resurrection, not the resurrection of Jesus Christ in particular, but the whole idea of resurrection. 'Nobody can be raised from the dead, therefore Christ was not raised from the dead' is their contention. In the first part of the chapter the form of the argument is decided by the way in which the problem has been raised. People have said there is no resurrection of the dead, just like that, and Paul explains to them that there must be a resurrection of the dead, because Christ Himself was raised from the dead; and he gives the evidence for that surprising statement.

This is, of course, the earliest evidence which we have of the Resurrection of Jesus Christ, and it comes from a long time before the Gospels. Paul claims, and obviously the claim must be a valid one, or else it would have been torpedoed long ago, that he received this from the early witnesses of the Resurrection, and that the Church had believed it from the very beginning. The evidence is pretty strong, you will notice, and not the least strong part of it is the statement that Jesus appeared after His death 'to five hundred of our brothers at once, most of whom are still alive, though some have died'. Now five hundred people is a very large number, and those who disbelieved the testimony were at liberty to ask any of the five hundred if it was true. 'Then he appeared to James, and afterwards to all the apostles.' It is sometimes said that Jesus appeared only to those who were His followers. That is a very doubtful statement. These five hundred were not all His followers, I suspect, at the time He appeared to them. Some of them were converted by the appearance. Then again James, presumably His brother, was almost certainly not a

Christian until after the Resurrection; when Jesus appeared to His brother he was not already persuaded, but was no doubt persuaded by the Resurrection. And, of course, Paul was not a Christian at the moment of Christ's appearance to him.

From verse 12 onwards Paul argues that the Resurrection of Jesus Christ indicates that there is a resurrection of the dead. If there were no resurrection of the dead we should be in despair, and those who have died in Christ are utterly lost; but in fact we are not driven to this desperate belief because Christ has been raised from the dead.

Then from verse 20 onwards he explains to us why the Resurrection of Jesus Christ involves our resurrection. He does not say, as sometimes he is quoted as saying, that because Christ rose, therefore we shall all rise. After all, Christ was the Son of God, and if the Son of God rises from the dead it does not follow that those of us who are not the Son of God will rise from the dead. Such an argument would obviously not be a strong one, but it is not the argument he uses. The argument he uses is really contained in verse 22: 'As in Adam all men die, so in Christ all will be brought to life'.

Remember what I said at the very beginning about the two communities, the community of Adam and the community of Christ. Membership of the Adam community involves death; membership of the Christ community involves resurrection. That is the point. We are not raised from the dead simply because Christ rose from the dead, but because we are *in Christ*, and those who are *in Christ* share His Resurrection. He is, as it were, the captain of our team, and we share the victory which He has won on our behalf. He is our champion, we are in Him; and what He has won is shared by us: 'As in Adam all men die, so in Christ all men will be brought to life.'

In that verse it is a little difficult to see what is meant by 'all': 'As in Adam *all* men die, so in Christ *all* men will be brought to life.' I suggest to you that this is not a statement that one day everybody will be resurrected. If everybody one day will be resurrected, it is a little difficult to see why the Gospel has to be preached at all! The statement is rather this: 'As in Adam all men die, for all men are in him, so all those who are in Christ will be brought to life.' Paul has put it rather loosely, but the statement he is making is that in the Adam community all men are doomed to death, and in the Christ community all those who belong to it are promised life. Christ, of course, has won the victory for all men, the offer is open to everybody, but there is no guarantee that all men will receive it.

'But each in his own proper place: Christ the first fruits, and afterwards, at his coming, those who belong to Christ.' Here we have to remember the situation in which Paul is writing. He believed that the Second Coming of the Lord would take place in the lifetime of most of those who were alive, a view which he gradually had to abandon and which does not really appear in his last epistles. But here he still believes it, and so he is describing the general resurrection in the terms of the Second Coming in the near future. If you bear that in mind, what he says here explains itself. So this means that those who have died in between, between now and the Coming of Christ, will be raised from the dead at His Coming to be with Him.

'Then comes the end, when he delivers up the kingdom to God the Father, after abolishing every kind of domination, authority, and power. For he is destined to reign until God has put all enemies under his feet'. The enemies of Christ will, at His coming in glory, be brought under His feet, and then death itself will be destroyed. And when all things have been made subject to Christ, the Son Himself will become subordinate to God, and God will be all in all. In the thought of Paul, Jesus is completely divine, but He is subordinate to the Father, because in the last analysis, in the last day of human history, Christ will acknowledge His subordination to the Father and the Father will be all in all.

But he is not quite satisfied that he has entirely proved his point, and he therefore goes back a bit. Remember that it is rather characteristic of Paul to bring forward an argument to its final conclusion and then go back to an earlier point in case some people have not been persuaded. It's not a very logical thing to do, and is not to be recommended in a sermon, but this is, after all, a letter and not a sermon.

He speaks of those who receive baptism on behalf of the dead. 'Why should they do this?' he asks. 'If the dead are not raised to life at all, what is the point of being baptized on their behalf?' This refers to a custom of the early Church, which Paul neither approves or disapproves, apparently. People whose relatives had died before the time of Christ or who had died without believing in Christ were anxious about them, naturally enough, and sometimes, apparently, were baptized as proxies for those who were already dead, and Paul says that this would be a quite useless custom if the dead were not raised.

Then he makes another point on the same lines. Why do we face dangers hour by hour if there is no resurrection of the dead? Why did he, Paul, fight wild beasts at Ephesus, if there was nothing to be gained by it? That is not an argument on the highest possible level. There is surely a value in heroism, there is a merit in courage and self-sacrifice, even if there is no life to come. We do not do good deeds because 'we hope for Heaven thereby'. But for the moment Paul uses the argument that there is no value in enduring hardship and danger if there is no life after death. He is really arguing with the Corinthians on their own level.

**15$^{33-4}$.** Here Paul argues against the hedonists, the people who say, 'Let us eat and drink, for tomorrow we die', and there have always been plenty of people who say that sort of thing, more especially in our own time. Paul argues against hedonism in Corinth by quoting one of the pagan poets, Menander, an Athenian writer of comedies, and points out that even the pagans believe in good character. In the light of this, he urges them to come back to a sober and upright life and to leave their sinful ways. This may be a digression from the main argument in order to bring in a pagan poet!

**15³⁵⁻⁵³.** 'How are the dead raised? In what kind of body?' Paul describes this as a senseless question—and then answers it at considerable length. The analogy which he uses is that of a seed sown in the ground. What he is saying in essence is this: ' When you sow a seed in the ground and in due course reap the harvest, the harvest which you reap is obviously not the same as the seed which you sow; nevertheless it is continuous with it and developed out of it. In the same way, this body which we have at the moment is not the same as that which will take part in the resurrection of the dead, but the body which will take part in the resurrection of the dead is continuous with our present body and developed out of it. Our resurrection body, therefore, is not the same as the body which we have now, but it is continuous with it, and it is something to which the Spirit has given a life which enables it to conquer that which we call death. It is a ' spiritual body '.

That is the essential position which he here maintains. He argues to it thus: ' " The first man, Adam, became an animate being ", whereas the last Adam has become a life-giving spirit. Observe, the spiritual does not come first; the animal body comes first, and then the spiritual.' He takes a passage in the Book of Genesis ('The first man, Adam, became an animate being ') to imply that the last man, the last Adam, must be the opposite, the last Adam must be a life-giving spirit. Remember that we mean by ' spiritual ' not, in a vague sense, ' that which is not earthly ', ' that which is not natural or fleshly '; we mean by ' spiritual ', ' that which is informed and infused by the Spirit of God '. So we come to the notion of the 'spiritual body'. Remember too what I have said several times about the word ' body ': the word ' body ' in St Paul does not simply mean the worldly, earthly part of us; it means our whole personality. What St Paul is saying is that in the resurrection we shall have our full personality, expressing itself through those organs of expression which God will provide for us, suitable for the life of Heaven. We shall not be inanimate ghosts, we shall not be spirits flitting from place to place, as sometimes people have thought. We shall be full personalities; we shall be bodies in whom the Spirit dwell, to whom the Spirit has given life. That is why we always have to say that the Christian doctrine of the life to come is not a doctrine of the immortality of the soul, but a doctrine of the resurrection of the body.

I fear that most Christians, if you were to ask them what they believed about the life to come, would say that they believed that our souls are immortal. You will not find any statement in the New Testament which gives colour to that. The statement in the New Testament is that our bodies will be resurrected. If you take that to mean the resurrection of the flesh, that this body which we now possess will be resuscitated at the last day, then of course it is obviously a very difficult thing to believe. Many people, thinking that they were required to believe that, have gone off to accept something else, a more congenial view that the soul is immortal, and have pretended that this is the Christian doctrine. But if you fully understand St Paul, you will see that he is not saying that this particular body will be resuscitated, but that we shall be given that full personality, with organs for the full expression of our powers and for communication with our fellow men, which is suitable to the life of Heaven, and you will agree with me that our present understanding of the human body and the human soul, and of the relationship between them, brings considerable support to what St Paul says. This is a matter on which modern psychology and St Paul are not at all difficult to reconcile. That does not prove that St Paul is right, of course, because modern psychology may say something different later! But it does make the idea a bit more congenial to modern thinkers. Anyway, our belief, according to St Paul, is in the resurrection of the body, and not the immortality of the soul.

The doctrine of the immortality of the soul is a view of very respectable origin; it goes back to the philosophy of Plato, and before that. But it does suggest that our bodies, our full personalities, are not of the stuff which endures, that we shall shed the physical part of ourselves and continue to exist as pure spirit or pure soul. The Hebrews didn't like the idea. They didn't think that there was any such thing as pure soul, or pure spirit. Soul or spirit to them always had to be embodied; there always had to be a relationship between the core of our being, and its expression and communication with others and its relation to others. So they did not hold with a soul which was immortal by itself. But perhaps the real condemnation of the doctrine of the immortality of the soul is that it is an individualistic doctrine. It suggests that eternity is inherited by individual disembodied spirits, and it lacks the full richness of the Christian view, according to which there is a communion of saints in which we still belong to each other, still communicate with each other, are still known to each other, still love each other, within the body of Christ in the world to come, even more fully and truly than in this present world.

**15$^{54-8}$.** If there were no such thing as sin, says Paul, there would be no sting in death. As you know, many of our contemporaries have given up belief in the life to come, and are quite happy at the prospect of annihilation, because they are not conscious of the power of sin, not conscious that sin has any serious consequences in the future. They are prepared to die, having lost both the belief in immortality and the belief in sin. For the sting of death is sin. If you believe in sin, then death has a sting, and sin gains its power from the law. ' But, God be praised, he gives us the victory through our Lord Jesus Christ.' Then, quite characteristically, Paul comes, as it were, off his high horse; he abandons his majestic language and comes down to plain everyday common sense: ' Therefore, my beloved brothers, stand firm and immovable, and work for the Lord always, work without limit, since you know that in the Lord your labour cannot be lost.'

A Christian doing his daily work, a Christian serving his Master in the ordinary intercourse of daily life, is certain that his labour is not lost, because he knows, he *knows*, that nothing in death or life can separate him from the love of God which is in Christ Jesus. For death is swallowed up and victory is won.

# QUESTIONS FOR DISCUSSION

*Study One*

(a) How can we be both ' in Christ ' and sinners at the same time?

(b) Are we in danger of making Christianity fit in with our preconceived ideas and social habits?

(c) How does the Holy Spirit teach us?

*Study Two*

(a) In view of St. Paul's teaching about the Church, can Christian divisions be defended?

(b) Is it true that every Christian has a ' gift of the Spirit '?

(c) Work out the meaning of Christian love in the most practical manner possible.

*Study Three*

(a) Is a Minister anything more than a full-time servant of the Church? If so, what is he?

(b) What are the main tasks of a Minister in relation to (i) God, and (ii) men?

(c) Do we give too much or too little authority to the Minister?

*Study Four*

(a) In what sense do sexual relations involve the whole personality?

(b) Is celibacy a right aim for some Christians?

(c) What is the Christian argument against extra-marital sexual relations?

*Study Five*
- (*a*) Ought Christians to go to law to protect their rights?
- (*b*) How far ought a Christian to compromise with the habits of his non-Christian acquaintances?
- (*c*) Should we dismiss the religion of 'heathens' as mere superstition?

*Study Six*
- (*a*) Do our services of Holy Communion preserve the spirit of the Lord's Supper in the time of St Paul?
- (*b*) Is there a place for both liturgical and 'free' worship in the same Church?
- (*c*) What emphasis ought preachers and teachers today to lay on the doctrine of the Resurrection?

www.ingramcontent.com/pod-product-compliance
Lightning Source LLC
Chambersburg PA
CBHW070517090426
42735CB00012B/2812